BROAD SCOPE: THE BENEFITS OF INTERDISCIPLINARY TRAINING FOR PEDAGOGY

Candice Rowser

TABLE OF CONTENTS

INTRODUCTION

Teaching history has helped me learn more concretely that it is an umbrella area of study- there is development over time in many aspects of existence. For example, with the study of evolution there is a joining of history, life science, earth science, zoology, or botany. It makes sense for history to be part of an interdisciplinary program, possibly the discipline that unites the others. Another thing that became even more evident to me was the fact that we live history and this is why it should never be eliminated from the curriculum at any level of education. This realization came through an activity that I have required of my college students - news presentations. The presentations have stimulated my desire to pay closer attention to current events (the present) than I had before. I hope the realization that we live history is one thing that students took away from my courses. With this work I want to showcase the broad ability one gains from receiving an interdisciplinary training. I would like to provide some information on my training and teaching experience.

My training in the Africana Studies Master's program at University at Albany, SUNY and Modern World History Doctor of Arts program at St. John's University equipped me with the ability to teach a broad range of courses. The nature of a "studies" program includes an examination or survey of the world, a world region, and a group of people, institution, or other phenomena through multiple avenues and fields of investigation. It allows one to have a scope from which he or she could teach, research, or practice depending on the field of work.

That graduate training enabled me to teach history and political science from the first semester I taught at the college level. In January of 2009 I interviewed and was hired to teach African-American history; two days later I was called with a question of whether or not I could teach World Politics, and I agreed to teach it. Though I specialize in World History, African History and African-American History I have regularly taught seven courses, four history and three political science: World History, African History, European History, African-American History, World Politics, American Government and

1

Politics, and Politics of Economics. What I have learned is there are some themes or topics that overlap and/or complement one another. When requested to teach courses that are not my specialty I have been able to teach them because I have had some basic exposure in relation to another subject area. As colleagues noted in their observation reports I have been effective.

After completing a workshop in 2013 the facilitator wrote notes to each participant, she noted in mine my pragmatic approach to teaching. Candidly I have grown frustrated with the idealized talk on teaching; I would say I am one that simply does or practices. The experiences I had along the way contribute to my pragmatic pedagogy. They helped me to make the necessary and reasonable adjustments to the reality of twenty-first century college students. Most of my experience in higher education has been at the two-year college through which I have learned most students in recent years work. It is not my philosophy to overload my students with work, what does that prove? When I think about my own student experience I remember being annoyed when finishing a course feeling like I did not really learn anything. I had been expected to produce so much that it left me no time to process. I want my students to PROCESS; that is what has guided me in my approach to instruction.

The foundation of the learning experience with me has been lecture periodically introduced or paused with questions to students. My rationale in doing this is: 1) for me to find out what they know, 2) I want them to see what they know or do not know, and 3) I want them to see how I can help fill in the blanks for them. As I am not well-versed in philosophy or outright educational theory, I have come to learn this is the Socratic Method (from the observation report of a senior colleague, Dr. Joseph Felser, at Kingsborough Community College, CUNY). I have encouraged my students to ask questions also. The rationale for this is for them to show their: 1) development of critical thinking, 2) ability to connect the dots, 3) attempts to master concepts, or 4) attempts at familiarizing themselves with historical facts.

Another vital aspect of the learning experience includes individual presentations during which students are discussion leaders. I have been explicit in telling them that during those presentations they are in fact teaching me as well. I have requested they bring in a news story that is connected to the course topic or theme (making the direct connection was a suggestion from my former professor and Chair, Dr. Mauricio Borrero, at St. John's University). Typically I thought of the topics when I assigned students to present because at times something has come up during the lecture, and I want a relevant and recent example or real world evidence. Initially the news was a part of only world themed courses like Emergence of Global Society (World History) at St. John's University and International Relations at Kingsborough Community College, CUNY. I later changed it to all three political science courses as it was a civic engagement activity, and then I required students in all of my courses to do them. Some students provided informal feedback on how they began paying closer attention to the news and how they better understood some of the political science concepts from class because they saw them practiced in the real world. I have also incorporated some of the facts from student presentations into my lectures, particularly when information included is from an official government agency, international organization, government official, or recent studies.

After about seven years of teaching I began opening all of my history courses by revisiting history as a field of study. In Ancient World History philosophy and history as areas of study, as we have come to see them in the modern world, are presented. I thought it was advantageous to students to have a clearer view of what history is and so I asked what is history? Most of the students that answered respond with it being a study of past events or some version of that. I then asked well who is at the center of those events? Most often students were confused, I guess, because they think it is a specific person or group of people. I eventually would say "people!" People are at the center of those past events. I anticipated this view of history would make it easier for them to process the information by not focusing so strongly on the dates but on the people.

3

Classification of Lectures Featured and Rationale

Included here are some lectures that fall into three basic categories of courses that most colleges and universities require for fulfillment of general education in humanities and social sciences. I titled them some general version of the categories, they are 1) World History, Affairs, and Cultures; 2) African and Diaspora History; 3) Political Science and Civic Engagement (the core of political science is civic engagement).

I want to provide the reasoning for selecting the lectures featured. Under the World category the "Age of Revolution" includes a series of events of which people living in the 21st century and beyond must have familiarity. This general event demonstrates that ideas (popularized during the Enlightenment) can turn into action and spark movements. It has also become apparent the need for the resurrection of ideas; this has been what I learned in teaching World History 2010-2011 and 2016-2018 and European History 1789-1945 (taught 2010-2016 which has events that overlap with World History). I am uncertain if students realized there is such a thing as the globalization of ideas. When I covered the rebellion in what became the United States (the government developed based on the idea of liberalism) a student asked if the Declaration of Independence was available online? That student stated that what is in the document is not what they observed happening in the U.S. Generations must be reminded of historical facts which optimistically would allow people to recognize the contradictions in society that initiate desire for change. We should have learned in the U.S. with the 2017-2021 administration how dangerous action without facts can be. Additionally, we should have learned it is intrinsic that we have facts, ideas, truth and knowledge of the past.

The "Age of Imperialism" is included as a major current in world history. In the process of presenting the historical facts I realized it is relevant to the current discussion and debate around immigration in the U.S. and Europe. During the time period covered (late 19th to early 20th centuries) the U.S. did not take part in the way Europe did, but there is a connection. This event was spurred, in part, by the Industrial

Revolution and the desire for natural resources to keep pace with the accelerated manufacturing capability. The implementation of a colonial administration was done to control and manage access to natural resources in other world regions. There was a manipulation of human resources (workers) in colonial territories in Asia and Africa to extricate natural resources to ship to Europe for manufacture into finished goods that would be sold on the global market. Not only did goods move across the world, but people moved too to labor in the factories that were built and became the heart of industrialization. We must revisit these series of events because we see and experience their remnants. Today people from those same continents migrate to Europe and the U.S. People decide to leave their home countries for better lives, usually this means they want to enhance their economic status with job or business opportunities. There is a correlation between the recent migrations globally and imperialism. Imperialism as part of industrialization led to a transfer of focus in the global economy by shifting the center of production to those countries that were among the first to industrialize. It can be argued that the natural resources more easily accessible then are difficult to attain today without advanced machinery. People today have a challenge in accessing natural resources in their home countries to transform into marketable goods to sell on the world market on their terms. As a result they search for other means of improving their economic positions by migrating to countries that play a dominant role in the global economy.

World Wars one and two from history and political science are part of major events in the 20th century. This was a time in human history when some people maximized humanity's capacity to take life, perhaps not envisioned before. Including the World Wars, the Cold War, and terrorism as discussed in political science shows the different type of analysis in the typing and quantification of recent conflict, not necessarily the series of events that resulted in the conflicts as history does. From the historical perspective we learn the impact of individuals in positions of influence on their countries. We learn about the rush to engage in conflict without a true assessment of the consequences. We learn about irony in that Austria was at the center of orchestrating diplomacy in

Europe during the 19th century, and in 1914, it had a sizable part of the responsibility for the world's most deadly war at the time. We come to know the mishaps in handling the aftermath of war and how missteps can play a role in the sentiments that lead to another war (dealing with Germany after World War I). We learn the danger of high production capacity to build up a military and how misguided ideas lead to deadly conflict.

In the wake of the deadliest wars of the 20th century major powers realized the need to cooperate to avoid war on such a scale. International organizations like the United Nations would play a part on the world stage and expand its role beyond keeping peace. Each continent during the second half of the 20th century also acknowledged the need to collaborate economically, so we see the founding of regional organizations also. It appears the name of the game for the global community since around 1950 is working together. There have been conflicts globally since that time, but none at the same level or scope of the World Wars.

For the Africa and Diaspora[1] History lectures I thought it was necessary to show that Black history as celebrated in the U.S. during the month of February did not simply begin on the shores of the U.S. in the 17th century, but goes back across the Atlantic to Africa. The societies and states in Africa are included in both Modern African History and African-American History. I open African-American History with the characteristics of those states and societies before and during the Trans-Atlantic Slave Trade. I want students to be familiar with the societies from which Africans in the old diaspora (in the Americas) originate. It is imperative to present realities of Africa before more frequent interactions with Europeans to illustrate the complexities of its peoples and institutions. African-American History and the stories of other members of the old African Diaspora are volumes in the overall collection of Africa's history, they just took place outside of the continent involuntarily. From student feedback that I requested in 2018 the connection between the African continent and African-Americans was executed successfully. They learned African societies were interrupted and African-Americans come from

---

[1] My exposure and focus is the diaspora in the Americas.

established communities constructed in ways that aligned with their ways of thinking, seeing the world, and being. The approximate four century Trans-Atlantic Slave Trade is the vehicle by which we get an old African Diaspora, enslaved African peoples dispersed to different countries in North and South America specifically.

Africa after decolonization is included to show Africa after its peoples and institutions were made subject to the European colonial experience. Those decades of colonialism, in most cases approximately eight to nine, were a time of interference for the peoples in the region; their economic activities were focused on outside actors and goals. Though there are advancements in recent years the colonial past remains palpable.

The Civil War and Reconstruction lecture should show there is residue in American society even in the twenty-first century from this event that has yet to be resolved appropriately. Something cannot be in the past if it is still present. There was an effort to discontinue the exploitation and dehumanization of Africans in America with a simultaneous push to devise a new means of keeping them enslaved. The second effort seems to have won. It was a challenge to teach this because of the inaccuracies presented at the earlier levels of school. Among the opinions from students' feedback was that African-American History should be required at all schools, it should not be optional as some acknowledged that it is in fact American history. Perhaps a valuable recognition for my students and me was which history is being taught, by whom, and how?

We can still see the residue of enslavement in the U.S. also in the experiences of African-Americans in education, the job market, and dealings with police. When enslaved Africans were brought to the U.S. they were to labor against their will, for no compensation, and for no benefit to themselves. It should come as no surprise there would be limited investment in educational institutions that would prepare them with skills beyond the work they had been forced to perform. Additionally, after the Civil War there were laws enacted in the South that aimed to keep African-Americans as close to

7

enslaved as possible. In recent years when African-Americans encounter obstacles in the job market it is clear there are continued efforts to keep them at the periphery of the American economy with limited means to build their own wealth. Alongside the impediments to a suitable living standard, lately the U.S. and world witnessed innumerable acts of brutality against African-Americans. We saw police killing African-American men by various means but there has been a rise in killing of African-American women (the lecture featured is an earlier version).

I have taught both African and African-American History to students of many ethnicities and recent immigrants to the U.S. and the general appreciation for the courses is universal. These courses involve the story of interactions between two general groups of humanity who work from different points of reference and a substantial part of the interaction involved atrocities. What students learn in the process and are frustrated by is what they see as an effort by society to not be truthful about those atrocities. As humanity we must deal with these historical realities.

The Political Science and Civic Engagement section includes one lecture from American Government and Politics and three lectures from Politics of Economics. Because of the recent events in the U.S., perusing social media and the traditional news, and talks with family and friends about their interactions on social media, I realize too many Americans are unfamiliar with the basics of their country's governmental structure and functioning. What is included is the earliest version of the lecture on the branches of government which over time I expanded. In expanding the lecture I simply incorporated instructor resources included in a number of recently published course textbooks (done for the World Wars history presentation topic also).

For Politics of Economics I included the lectures explaining government and economics to show the connection of the two spheres. It is critical to comprehend the relationship because inept members of government can harm the economy; the 2007-2008 recession and Covid-19 response present us recent examples of the consequences of a hands-off approach from the government. It seemed necessary to include the macroeconomics or national economy lecture because of limitations of knowledge in this area also. The government has a role in the national economy and the more citizens understand that as well as the way the government works, the better. We can make different choices for members of the body that makes decisions for us and manages things on our behalf (the government).

SECTION 1 WORLD HISTORY, AFFAIRS, AND CULTURES

WORLD HISTORY

AGE OF REVOLUTION

The "Age of Revolution" theme/topic is part of four courses: Modern World History, European History, American Government and Politics, and Politics of Economics. The ideas that sparked changes in society were expanded upon and circulated more widely at that time, though that circulation beyond the elite class was unanticipated. These events serve as lessons for today; from student comments and questions it appears they understood the lessons too. For the four courses this theme was covered slightly differently; for the political science courses the focus was more on the theorists of government while the World History course had a broader coverage. For the Politics of Economics course included were some brief points on economics.

THE ENLIGHTENMENT

- Europe during the 17th & 18th centuries.
- It was an intellectual and cultural movement & a state of mind.
- Influenced by the Scientific Revolution (occurred same time) methods were applied to human nature & human affairs.
- Centered in France, but active in other countries, popularized science & stressed reason to disprove faith and superstitious thinking.
- Why France? (1) Wealthiest & most populous country, (2) international language of the educated, (3) lower level of censorship compared to eastern and east-central European countries.
- Key people: John Locke, Baron de Montesquieu, Jean-Jacques Rousseau, Immanuel Kant, Denis Diderot, and David Hume.

- Called philosophes (French for philosopher OR free thinker).

WHAT IS PHILOSOPHY OR TO BE EDUCATED?

- Philosophes - some of them were intellectuals not formally trained or connected to educational institutions.

- Philosophes extended & popularized each other's ideas.

- Popularized new ideas, methods of investigation, and views of educational theory.

- Catholic Church as feudal authority, rejected at the time.

- Basic idea - rational laws were applicable to social & physical behavior.

- Enlightenment thinkers believed in the natural goodness & rationality of humans.

- Progress in knowledge convinced them that more human growth was possible too.

- Began revolutionary developments in art, philosophy, & politics.

- It set the stage for modern political movements, from liberalism → socialism.

- Social sciences developed at this time → political science, psychology, sociology& economics.

- Peculiar reality of the time → this movement not directed toward the masses → peasants, urban workers. Educated elite thought they lacked the time and talent for philosophical debate.

- Led to reading revolution, the father read to family to now individual silent reading. The production and sale of religious books declined while books & pamphlets on history, law, arts, and sciences rose. Prices of books decreased.

- Led to development of spaces and tools for discussion, debate, critical thinking → became popular.

- CENTERS FOR PHILOSOPHICAL DISCUSSION
  Late 1600s coffee houses, salons (rooms in elite homes) book clubs, masonic lodges, journals.

JOHN LOCKE (1632-1704)

- Studied experimental science & medicine at Christ Church, Oxford 1652, graduated 1656, earned a Master's 1658.
- Two Treatises of Government (1690)
- Argued: in the natural state people were equal and independent.
- Everyone has the right to defend "life, liberty, and property."
- People agree (contract) to form society with a governing body to protect everyone and their property.
- Government is created after people have agreed to give over power to specific officers.
- Governmental powers are limited and can be changed by the people.

BARON DE MONTESQUIEU (1689- 1755)

- Spirit of the Laws (1748)
- Inquiry into the structures that shaped law.
- Question: how did different environments, histories, customs, and religious traditions combine to create a variety of governmental institutions?
- What "spirit" (idea, view, and principle) characterized each form of government?
- What were their virtues (pros) and shortcomings (cons)?
- Proposed threefold classification of states:
- Republic: governed by the many (elite aristocracy or the people)

- Monarchy: 1 single authority ruled in accordance with the law
- Despotism: allowed 1 single ruler to govern unchecked by law or other powers
- Admired the British system & its separate & balanced powers - executive, legislative, judicial → guaranteed freedom from absolute power of any single individual or group.
- "Checks & balances"

JEAN-JACQUES ROUSSEAU (1712- 1778)

- The Social Contract (1762)
- "Man was born free, and everywhere he is in chains?"
- What were the origins of government?
- Was government's authority legitimate?
- Social inequality, rooted in private property corrupted the "social contract," or formation of government.
- Under these conditions, government & laws represented only the rich & privileged → Instruments of oppression & enslavement.
- Legitimate authority derived from the people alone → POPULAR SOVEREIGNTY
- Argued 3 points:
- 1st sovereignty shouldn't be divided among 3 branches of government or rest in a king.
- 2nd exercising sovereignty changed the nations - when individual citizens formed a "body politic," it became more than simply the sum of its parts.
- Citizens are bound by mutual obligation & not force.
- 3rd the national community will be united by the "general will" → equality of common interests.
- BIRTHED THE IDEOLOGIES OF NATIONALISM & SOCIALISM
- Government: organization of individuals who have the power to make binding decisions on behalf of a particular community.

Political movements influenced by Enlightenment ideas

AMERICAN REVOLUTION/REBELLION 1775-1781

- Britain, under King George III, began imposing a series of taxes on colonists in British North America, in an attempt to deal with debt and the cost of maintaining empire.
- George Grenville (1712-1770) British Prime Minister 1763-1765 who implemented the tax policies that sparked opposition in the North American colonies.
- Colonists argued that they should have representation in government if they were going to be taxed.
- Englishmen had the right to be taxed only by their elected representatives.
- Colonists were not represented in British Parliament and so claimed they should not pay taxes.
- Taxes that sparked opposition:
- Sugar Act 1764: taxed sugar, coffee, wine, and other items.
- Stamp Act 1765: taxed most printed material newspapers, pamphlets, leases, deeds, licenses, college diplomas, even playing cards. (Main Target of Colonists' Protest).
- Quartering Act 1765: stated that colonists must provide food, drink, fuel, places to sleep, and transportation to British soldiers.
- Townshend Acts 1767 (new Finance Minister Charles Townshend 1725-1767): taxed glass, lead, paper, paint, and tea. Stated the New York Assembly must go along with the Quartering Act or they could not meet.
- Intolerable Acts 1774: closed Boston harbor until tea lost during the Boston Tea Party was paid for. (£15,000). Made Massachusetts a crown colony and set up a military government.
- British colonists made preparations for self-government.
- September 5, 1774, the First Continental Congress assembled in Philadelphia, PA with 55 members elected by provincial congresses representing 12 continental

- colonies, except Georgia, Quebec, Nova Scotia, and the Floridas.
- The purpose was to deliver a series of solutions and protests.
- The Continental Congress adopted the Continental Association of 1774 that recommended that every county, town, and city form committees to enforce a boycott on all British goods.
- King George III responded by declaring the colonies in a state of rebellion.
- James Wilson of Pennsylvania and Thomas Jefferson of Virginia wrote two pamphlets that were spread widely.
- Wilson wrote Considerations on the Nature and Extent of the Legislative Authority of the British Parliament.
- Jefferson wrote Summary View of the Rights of British America.
- They argued in both that the colonies were not subject to Parliament, but only the crown, and that each colony was a separate domain.
- April 1775, British and British colonists engaged in armed conflict in the Battles of Lexington and Concord starting the war.
- The Second Continental Congress assembled in Philadelphia on May 10, 1775.
- June 7, 1776, Richard Henry Lee of Virginia proposed a resolution that "these United Colonies are, and of right ought to be, free and independent states…" It passed on July 2, 1776.
- July 4, 1776, the Congress adopted Thomas Jefferson's Declaration of Independence drawn from John Locke's ideas.
- October 1781, Battle of Yorktown, Virginia and American victory.
- 1783 Treaty of Paris: formally ended the Revolutionary War and Britain recognized the United States' independence.

- King Louis the XVI (1754-1793) continued absolute rule of King Louis XIV (1638-1715). Louis XVI did not allow criticism of himself or his policies.
- He imprisoned anyone who did so without trial. The imprisonment was carried out by lettres de cachet or letters with the royal seal.
- He was an ineffective leader.
- French population was divided into 3 groups:
  - First Estate: Clergy
  - Second Estate: Nobles
  - together 3-5% of population
  - Third Estate: City-workers, peasants, bourgeoisie (bankers, businesspeople, professional people and middle class people) 95-97% of population.

Political Issues

- The Estates-General was the law making body where each estate had one vote.
- The Third Estate had very little voice in government.
- The Third Estate felt powerless because the other two estates voted together.

Economic Issues

- The Third Estate was heavily taxed, including a land tax and labor on roads.
- The Bourgeoisie's commercial enterprises were restricted.

Social Issues

- The First and Second Estate enjoyed more privileges than the Third.
- They owned most of the land and were exempt from taxes.
- 1789 King Louis XVI called the Estates-General to meet, which had not met since 1614 (175 years before). He wanted money to solve the financial crisis France faced.

- The Third Estate refused to accept the established voting method and demanded all 3 estates meet together and each deputy have a vote, the King refused.
- June 17, 1789 the Third Estate declared itself a National Assembly promised to write a national constitution in the Tennis Court Oath.
- They passed the Declaration of the Rights of Man and the Citizen on August 27, 1789.
- The Declaration of the Rights of Man :
  - Ended the class structure and privileges associated with the 3 estates.
  - Declared that people were equal before the law and had basic freedoms: freedom of religion, speech, and the press.
- 1790 National Assembly abolished the special taxes and privileges of the Catholic Church in the Civil Constitution of the Clergy.
- 1791 the French Constitution was written that created a constitutional or limited monarchy, and established separate branches of government: executive, legislative, and judicial.
- 1792 National Convention declared France a republic.
- 1793 Louis XVI was tried and executed.
- Fall of the Bastille July 14, 1789
- Brought about a fundamental change in the relationship between the government and those governed.
- Advanced democracy by acknowledging the individual's value and worth.
- Political power passed from an absolute monarch and nobles to the people.

HAITI & SOUTH AMERICA

1791-1830

CARIBBEAN BASIN- HAITI

- By the end of the 17th century Spain ceded the western third of Hispaniola to France and was named Saint-Domingue.

17

- In the 18th century French settlers established sugar plantations there and imported enslaved Africans to work them.
- The French setup a rigid social structure of French, creoles, freed Blacks and Black slaves.
- Haiti became France's most prosperous colony and the world's lead producer of sugar and coffee.
- Mulattoes revolted when creoles refused mulatto representation in the local assemblies & the French National Assembly of 1789.
- In the 1790s, enslaved Africans in Haiti under the leadership of Francois-Dominique Toussaint L'Ouverture (the opening) fought against the French.
- In 1793, the British took over all of Haiti's coastal cities as part of their campaign against Napoleon.
- L'Ouverture recaptured them. In 1801, he declared himself emperor, abolished slavery, and initiated reforms.
- Napoleon sent troops to Haiti, but they couldn't capture the interior. U.S. President Thomas Jefferson sent aid to the rebels to protect against an invasion of Louisiana.
- Haiti gained independence 1804, became the second nation to win independence in the Western hemisphere, and the first Black republic.

SOUTH AMERICAN REVOLUTIONS

- Discontent was evident in the late 18th century.
- Indigenous peoples and mestizos (mixed Spaniard and indigenous) fought against limited freedom and harsh treatment.
- Revolts broke out in Peru and spread to Colombia in the 1770s, but were defeated by military force and deception.
- Those who revolted attacked the estates system and high taxes imposed by the Spanish administration.
- Creoles (Spaniards born in South American colonies) had problems with the structure of society.

- They lacked political power because they were excluded from participating in the administration. Only the peninsulares (born in Spain) had power.
- Early in the 18th century Creoles were part of the colonial administration, but after 1750 Spain got rid of the Creoles' role.
- Creoles faced heavy economic restrictions and taxes.
- The first part of the war for independence was in Venezuela 1810, when the Caracas city council debated over loyalty to the Napoleonic regime in Spain.
- King Ferdinand's government declared the new regimes in revolt and ordered the leaders' deaths.
- The new administration in Venezuela formed its own army and declared its independence in 1811.
- Spanish forces put down the regime in 1812.
- A wealthy Creole, Simón Bolívar, gathered an army of former British, Irish, and German soldiers, Creole nationalists, and indigenous troops.
- In 1819 Bolivar defeated the Spanish army, proclaimed a new republic called Gran Colombia (a union of Venezuela and Colombia).
- Bolivar's armies invaded Ecuador adding it to Gran Colombia.
- In 1810, independence movements occurred further south.
- In Buenos Aires a temporary government was set up under the leadership of a Creole General José de San Martín, an army organized.
- The army established a full government in Argentina (1816) and helped Chile's movement for independence.
- Priests Miguel Hidalgo and José Morelos led a lower-class rebellion of Spanish speaking indigenous Americans and mestizos against the hacienda system in 1810 in Mexico.
- Creole Mexicans maintained loyalty to Spain until 1820, but a weakened Spain convinced the Creole elite they should take care of their own affairs in 1821.
- A conservative Mexican emperor, Agustín de Iturbide, was crowned in 1822.

- Creole defense of their elite position limited social impact of freedom movements.
  - They didn't intend to redistribute property & reconstruct society.
  - They rejected authority of the Spanish crown.
- Independence for colonies in Central America centered in Guatemala, where a United Provinces of Central America was declared in 1823.
- Under the threat of Napoleonic rule, the Portuguese King Joao fled to Brazil, but returned to Portugal in 1815.
- His son Pedro remained regent. Portugal tried to impose colonial control over Brazil again.
- Brazilian leaders wanted to maintain their Rio de Janeiro based government.
- Pedro joined this movement and declared Brazilian independence in 1822, with him as emperor.

Economic changes inspired by the Enlightenment ideas

INDUSTRIAL REVOLUTION (IR)

- The Industrial Revolution's beginnings were in England after 1750.

- Changes in agricultural practices → techniques, crops, and property holding. More food led to more people being fed with less labor which led to lower prices. This wealth went into investments in industry.

- Major shift in technology & power sources (before – wind & water after- coal & steam).

- Change from man & animal power → machine power.

- Power sources were applied to manufacturing → much faster production & increase in finished products.

- Goods were no longer manufactured in homes or small shops, but now in factories. FACTORY – most visible sign of the IR + centralization of production.

Industry = human quality, hard workers → industrious

After industry = economic system that follows its own logic independent of humans.

5 NECESSITIES OF INDUSTRIALIZATION

- *Natural resources* (England coal, iron ore, cotton, navigable rivers, canal system)

- *Labor force*

- *Available capital* (profits from trade + cottage industry)

- *Available markets* (overseas colonies)

- *Favorable government* (passed laws to protect private property, grants to investors, $ to build roads, canals, railroads.)

- Britain was able to cheaply produce goods in greatest demand → cotton clothes 40% of Brit exports.

- Production couldn't keep pace with demand → led to push to create new ways of manufacturing → machines.

- Several inventions contributed to the speed with which products were manufactured. Men wove cloth by using spinning wheels and hand looms.

- John Kay → flying shuttle 1733.

- James Hargreaves → *spinning jenny* 1764 spin yarn. Before women spun thread and yarn.

- Edmund Cartwright →*power loom* 1787 cloth weaving.

- James Watt improved the *steam engine* in the 1760s, but enhanced it in 1782 to drive machinery.

- 1799 Samuel Compton → spinning mule combined the jenny & frame.

- Engines were used in textile manufacturing, metallurgy, & coal mining - focus early phase of the revolution.

- Engines were used in sugar refining & printing.

- The American invention of interchangeable parts, first used for rifle manufacturing, helped machine building.

- Technological inventions impacted communication & transportation also.

- The development of the telegraph, steam shipping, & railway, early 19th century increased speed in transport of information & goods.

- Richard Trevithick invented the 1st steam-powered locomotive in 1804. Used on a rail line in southern Wales.

- 1st public rail lines opened in 1830 and was 32 miles from Manchester to Liverpool used George Stephenson's engine "Rocket."

- The railroad was an important contribution → faster transportation, prices fell, markets grew, and sales increased, more factories, more machinery → IR was self-supporting.

- By 1840 England had almost 6,000 miles of railroad. Railroad contribution created jobs.

- Technological developments reached offices & homes also with inventions like typewriters, cash registers, sewing machines, and refrigerators.

- Factories required workers to be disciplined & develop or have specialized skills.

- After 1850, corporations grew to sell shares to investors.

- The position that Western nations gained in the world economy offered the context for the Industrial Revolution.

- European nations acquired large sums of capital from their colonial trading activities, including the slave trade.

- Businessmen learned that there were markets for manufactured goods - find new & cheaper ways to make such goods. Production had to match demand.

- A massive population increase forced workers to take factory jobs because there was no alternative. Mostly peasants from rural areas, now obligated to work regular hours.

- It was better to bring workers to the machines, organize their labor in factories next to rivers, streams (power sources of early machines). FACTORY.

- New ideas & business mentality made some industrial entrepreneurs introduce risky changes.

- Material resources & capital were other areas where the West had advantages.

- CAPITALISM: Economic system in which the means of production & distribution are privately owned.

- The most important element is profit.

- Focus on individual effort/enterprise.

- Property- owners of the means of production (factories, land, tools, and machines) are called capitalists.

THE MIDDLE CLASS

- The French & Industrial Revolutions removed the hierarchies based on rank & privilege.
- They gave rise to new distinctions based on wealth or social class.
- The middle class became important.
- Another term for middle class was bourgeoisie which originally meant "city (Bourg) dweller" which included merchants, officials, artisans (skilled manual workers), lawyers, and men of letters (intellectuals).
- Entrepreneurs → factory & mine owners benefited most from IR. People who built factories, bought machines,

determined market location → possessed qualities like resourcefulness, vision, ambition, initiative, and greed.

- Term became applicable to people in commerce, industry, banking, professionals (teachers, physicians, government officials) regardless of residence.
- Very few people moved from the working class into the middle class.
- Upward mobility was almost impossible without education, and education - rare luxury for working-class children.
- Careers open to talents (a French Revolution goal) meant opening jobs to middle class young men who could pass exams.
- Support itself with the belief that it was possible to get ahead by intelligence & dedication to work.
- Claim to political power & cultural influence because they made up a new & deserving social elite, superior to common people, but different from the old aristocracy.
- Middle class attitude was controlled by "respectability."
- Values were important →
- Financial independence, providing responsibly for the family, and staying away from debt.
- The middle class held merit and character high as opposed to aristocratic privilege and living off of noble estates.
- These ideas were goals, not realities.
- Upper middle class → business families. Middle-middle class law & medical professionals, merchants, industrialists. Low-middle class → independent shopkeepers, small traders, and tiny manufacturers.

THE WORKING CLASS

- The working class was divided into different groups based on skill, wage, gender, & workplace.
- For example a skilled textile worker lived a different life than a ditch digger.

24

- The skilled textile worker could afford food, shelter, and clothing while the ditch digger struggled.
- Working class housing was quite unhealthy.
- Overcrowding was a major problem.
- The family was a survival system in which every member played a role.
- Wives had to earn wages & were expected to house, feed, and clothe the family on very little money.
- Working women's daily routine included
- Rounds of carrying & boiling water
- Cleaning
- Cooking
- Laundry
- This was done in one- & two-room crowded, unventilated, poorly lit apartments.

WORK FOR THE WORKING CLASS

- 12-16 hour days 6 days weekly. 30 minutes lunch and dinner each. No job security, minimum wage, unemployment benefits, workers' compensation, health benefits, sick time.
- Worse working conditions in the cotton mills – dirty, dusty, hot temperatures, unhealthy.
- Coal mines tunnels were 3-4 ft. high, dangerous conditions → cave-ins, explosions, gas fumes, deformities dampness led to lung problems.
- Men dug for coal, women and children pulled carts to lifts.
- 1821 50% British population under 20 yrs. old.
- 1830 women and children 2/3 of labor force in cotton industry. Women paid ½ of men's wages.
- 1838 29% of labor force younger than 18, as young as 7 years old working. Paid 1/6 – 1/3 of a man's wage.
- Labor movement began 1820s 1830s. England legalized trade unions in 1824 elsewhere in Europe around 1850. EX Amalgamated Society of Engineers (England) 1851 largest and most successful union. Right to strike came in the 1870s.

- FACTORY ACT OF 1833 → child workers 9-13 years old 8 hour days, 14-18 year olds 13 hours a day. 9 years old and younger went to schools set up by factory owners.
- Low wages, shortage of male labor, increase in white collar worker demand brought more women into work force as office workers→ typists, secretaries, file clerks, and sales clerks.

SOCIALISM

- Began in France after 1815 associated with idea of equality. Replace competition with cooperation.
- Socialism: supported the development of a cooperative community as opposed to fragmented, individualistic, competitive society.
- Henri de Saint Simon (1760-1825)
- Charles Fourier (1772-1837)
- French socialism pushed for 3 things:
- 1- planning
- 2- economic equality
- Gov. control of property
- Socialism has been associated mostly w/ KARL MARX (1818-1883)
- Communist Manifesto (1848)
- German thinker that promoted the idea of communism & socialism.
- Communism → economic system in which a single party controls the means of production with the goal of creating a classless society.
- Socialism → a system of social organization where the means of production and distribution (of capital and land) were held by the community.
- Argued that capitalism involves too much exploitation.
- Working class or proletariat will eventually revolt against the capitalists.
- Result of the revolution would be a utopian like society, one without classes.
- 1875 German Social Democratic Party emerged → passed laws to improve work conditions, by 1912 it became the largest party in Germany.

AGE OF IMPERIALISM

The "Imperialism" theme/topic is part of four courses: World History, World Politics, African History, and European History. I have shown a film for this topic so I only introduce it with the definition, causes, methods, and forms of imperialist control.

- Defined as control by one nation over another area or nation, usually one that is not as militarily strong.
- Areas under control are called colonies.
- The practice of imperialism can be referred to as colonialism.
- There are 2 periods of imperialism:

  - "Old Imperialism" 1500-1800

  - "New Imperialism" began in the 1880s

CAUSES

- With the successes gained from the Industrial Revolution, Europeans needed new markets and products to fuel their economies.
- Trade alone was not sufficient when new market agriculture, transportation systems, and areas of investments had to be created.
- The pioneering experience and success of the Industrial Revolution also contributed to European and North American development of a sense of superiority.
- There was also the desire to "bring civilization" to the world's peoples as defined by Europeans.
- Pressure for conquest developed after 1870, the belief was that every piece of available territory should be claimed as quickly as possible for national security and national glory.

METHODS

- Growth in technology played a major role in European imperialism throughout the world.

- European steam-powered ships were able to navigate African rivers that were impenetrable before.
- Advanced weaponry was another area in which Europeans were able to engage in conquest.
- Colonialists played on existing divisions (ethnic, social, religious) in the societies they conquered.

FORMS OF IMPERIALIST CONTROL[2]

- Sphere of influence:

  - A nation gained economic power in a region and had exclusive economic rights to trade, to invest, and to develop mines, railroads, or factories.

- Concession:

  - A foreign nation obtained special privileges. An underdeveloped area gave permission to a technologically advanced nation to do something of economic value in the area.

- Protectorate:

  - A colonial nation allowed the native ruler of an area to remain in office as a figurehead, while in reality the colonial power made all the major decisions.

- Colony:

  - An imperialist nation takes total control over an area and makes it part of its empire.

INDIA

- British conquest of India was completed by the 1st half of the 19th century.

---

[2] Barron's Global History and Geography Regents Review. Barron's Educational Series, 2006.

- Initially India was controlled by the East India Company, but later the British government assumed control.
- British officials' respect for Indian culture weakened, in their eyes India became a place to westernize.
- British rule allowed a degree of autonomy for specific areas where regional princes were allowed to keep governments under British advisors.
- A uniform code of law was enforced on the entire country.
- British colonial administration became larger and more proficient with direct taxes based on land values.
- The British established a civil service based on an examination system. The top officials were British until 1864. Lower-level officials were Hindus.
- British funded school system was created to teach Western values. Subjects were taught in English which became a second language among the upper-caste Hindu and Muslim leaders.
- The British aimed to make changes economically, socially, and politically with both success and failure.
- During the 1850s, they began to construct railroads and telegraph systems to facilitate administration and military control of the country. Industrial development was limited.
- The British tried to change the caste system, conditions for women, female infanticide, sati, and marriage laws (allowing widows to remarry).
- Resistance against British rule grew, especially to tax collection.
- Upper-caste Indians disliked the British opposition to the caste system.
- Hindu and Muslim Indians questioned the Christian missionary efforts and parts of the education system.
- This resistance led to the Sepoy Rebellion of 1857, when Indian soldiers thought that rifle bullets were being greased with animal fat. Hindus suspected beef fat was being used, while Muslim thought that pork fat was being used- for both groups extremely offensive.
- British reinforcements put down the uprising in 1858.

- Educated Indians, influenced by Western political and educational values, articulated a resistance to undemocratic foreign rule.
- The 1st Indian National Congress, with both Hindu and Muslim representatives (mostly civil servants), met in 1885.
- They demanded greater opportunities for Indians in the imperial bureaucracy.
- They also focused on creating an India that could industrialize on its own.
- The masses of Indians favored traditional ways and negatively viewed change (taxes, low paid labor).

CHINA

- From the 1820s on, Western traders became insistent on gaining access to Chinese markets and products.
- New demand for Chinese vases, porcelain, and other artifacts increased as a result of the growing wealth in Europe.
- This was the same time that the Qing dynasty was in decline: inefficient bureaucracy, weakened army, peasant uprisings.
- The Chinese government needed Western military support to conquer the Taiping rebels in the 1850s.
- The Opium War (1839-1842) was the 1st clash between the weakening Chinese empire and the West.
- British merchants in India had been exporting opium for sale in China, though they still had a problem finding goods that appealed to the Chinese market.
- The Chinese empire objected to the opium trade because the harmful effects (addiction) of it were well known.
- The government attempted to seize all opium in Canton (Guangzhou) harbor and prohibit all British trade in the area; this led to a fight with British sailors.
- War followed with the British blockading the entire coast. The Chinese couldn't fight because they had no effective navy.
- The Treaty of Nanking 1842 officially ended the war and required:

- The Chinese pay for all the British property they destroyed.
- They opened several ports to British merchants including Canton and Shanghai.
- They also gave the British the island of Hong Kong.
- The French and U.S. followed suit, demanding new trading rights.
- By 1850, foreign colonies existed in a number of ports.
- In 1857, a 2nd war led to the opening of more ports allowing Westerners to trade and engage in missionary activities.
- The Chinese government also struggled to deal with an increasing population.
- Some Chinese peasants were recruited by railroad bosses in the U.S. and parts of South America.
- Small groups of Chinese converted to Christianity which increased interest in Western ways.
- Western business activity helped further economic development regionally → population and wealth of the ports grew.
- Western governments favored a weak imperial administration to complete disorder.
- The Qing dynasty became more dependent on European, British, help during the 2nd half of the 19th century.
- At the same time, the government wanted to restore the emperor's reputation and traditional Confucian principles.
- The government tore up rail lines in the 1870s in an effort to maintain traditional ways.
- This was a clear indication of the desire to stay away from westernization.
- Economic change occurred in China's port cities because of Western influence, but most manufacturing continued with traditional, hand-labor methods.

AFRICA

- European interest in Africa increased as the slave trade no longer provided easy profits.

- The British and French in West Africa, over time acquired new territories.
- The British took over the city of Lagos in present day Nigeria, while the French controlled Dakar, in present-day Senegal.
- In southern Africa, migration of Boers (Dutch) settlers from the Cape Province spread when Britain obtained control of the Cape from Holland during the Napoleonic Wars (1799-1815).
- New imperialism came into full force after 1870.
- At the 1884-1885 Berlin Conference, Britain, France, Belgium, and Germany claimed territories in Africa without the presence of any leader from Africa.
- They agreed that traders and missionaries should have free access to the African interior.
- The slave trade should be abolished.
- European morality should be brought to Africans.
- European extended presence in Africa came along with insensitivity to local customs when imperialists tried to export or destroy religious symbols and ceremonial mechanisms.
- Example: A British governor incited a war when he tried to take the traditional Golden Stool of the Ashanti King to send to Queen Victoria.
- Resistance to European intrusion was severely crushed. Example: German massacre of tens of thousands of Africans.
- Britain → Malaya, Thailand, Burma, Ghana, Nigeria, Sierra Leone, Zambia, Zimbabwe, Cape Colony, Kenya, Uganda, Egypt, Sudan, Hong Kong, Singapore, Australia, New Zealand.
- Germany → Tanganyika, Namibia, Cameroon, Togo.
- France → Indochina (present-day Vietnam, Laos, Cambodia) Morocco, French West Africa - Senegal, Ivory Coast, Upper Volta (present-day Burkina Faso) Mali, Niger, Algeria, French Equatorial Africa (present-day Central African Republic, Repub. of the Congo, Gabon), Madagascar.
- The Netherlands → Indonesia, Transvaal and Orange Free State (present-day South Africa).

GLOBAL CONFLICT IN THE 20TH CENTURY

This theme/topic is part of World History, Europe: 1789 – 1945, and International Relations. In International Relations the presentation is more abridged because included are the categories of conflicts. In the presentation emphasis was on the lessons of the conflicts because when one thinks about it they could have been avoided.

WORLD WAR I

- Small countries in southeastern Europe helped to spark the outbreak of war after the reduction of the Ottoman Empire.
- Nationalism brought the emergence of new nations in southeastern Europe.
- Greece won independence in 1830; Serbia and Romania won their independence after the Congress of Berlin in 1878.
- 1903, Serbia became hostile toward Austria-Hungary and the Ottoman Empire.
- Driven by nationalism, Slavic Serbs wanted to join with Slavic Russians to form a new nation.
- 1908, Austria annexed Bosnia and Herzegovina (both have large Serbian, Croatian, and Muslim populations).
- Two nationalist wars, the First and Second Balkan Wars in 1912 and 1913, destroyed Ottoman presence in Europe.
- Austria-Hungary feared it would follow in being broken apart.
- Heir to the Austrian-Hungarian throne, Archduke Francis Ferdinand, and his wife, Sophie, were assassinated by nationalist Serbian revolutionaries June 28, 1914 during a state visit to Sarajevo, the Bosnian capital.
- Austria- Hungary's leaders presented Serbia with an ultimatum on July 23; they gave the Serbs 48 hours to agree to demands of Austrian control.

- Serbia replied vaguely, Austrian response was declaration of war on Serbia July 28.
- Germany's Emperor Wilhelm II and his chancellor, Theobald von Bethmann-Hollweg, supported Austria-Hungary.
- Germany hoped Russia and France would join in, but that Britain would be neutral.
- Diplomacy took a backseat; on July 28, Austrian armies attacked Belgrade, Serbia. Tsar Nicholas II ordered a partial mobilization against Austria-Hungary.
- July 29, Russia ordered full mobilization and declared general war against Austria-Hungary and Germany.
- Germany prepared to attack France through neutral Belgium before heading for Russia.
- August 2, 1914, General Helmuth von Moltke demanded Belgium allow German armies to pass through Belgian territory. Belgium refused.
- Germany invaded France through Belgium on August 3, 1914.
- Britain joined France and declared war on Germany August 4, 1914 → the start of World War I.

War Participants
- ALLIED POWERS→
- Britain, France, Russia, United States, Italy, Japan
- CENTRAL POWERS →
- Austria-Hungary, Bulgaria, Germany, Ottoman Empire

- Austria-Hungary surrendered on November 3, 1918.
- Germany's Emperor, Wilhelm II, stepped down and fled to Holland.
- Socialist leaders in Berlin declared Germany a republic on November 9 and agreed to Allied terms of surrender.
- A peace agreement went into effect November 11, 1918 which ended the war.

Treaty of Versailles:
- The peace conference was held at Versailles Palace near Paris January 1919.
- There were 70 delegates from 27 nations.

34

- The three dominant nations were the United States, Britain, and France.
- President Woodrow Wilson represented the U.S., Lloyd George represented Britain, and George Clemenceau represented France.
- President Wilson of the U.S. made a peace proposal, the Fourteen Points that stressed national self-determination and rights of small countries.
- President Wilson was adamant about creating a League of Nations (1919 - 1946).
- He thought that only a permanent international organization could protect member states from aggression and avoid future wars.
- Clemenceau and Lloyd George were more concerned with punishing Germany.
- Clemenceau wanted to demilitarize Germany and require payment of reparations.
- Germany's colonies went to France, Britain, and Japan.
- Alsace-Lorraine was returned to France.
- Parts of Germany inhabited by Poles were given to the new Polish state.
- The treaty limited Germany's army to 100,000 men and permitted no military defense in the Rhineland.
- Germany had to pay reparations for civilian damages resulting from the war.
- June 28, 1919, after protesting, Germany signed the treaty in the Hall of Mirrors at Versailles.
- Allies made separate treaties with the other defeated nations- Austria, Hungary, Bulgaria, and Turkey.
- Hungary's captive areas were given to Romania, Czechoslovakia, Poland, and Yugoslavia.
- Italy received some Austrian territory.
- The Ottoman Empire was broken up, with Lebanon and Syria going to France. Iraq and Palestine went to Britain, which included a Jewish national homeland promised by Britain in 1917.

- Fascism:
- Came as a result of World War I.
- Many supporters, former veterans, criticized the failures of parliamentary democracy and Western capitalism's corruption.
- To replace these political and economic structures, they suggested a strong state ruled by a powerful leader with a strong foreign and military policy.
- The first fascist regime rose in Italy 1923.
- The National Socialist or Nazi Party arose in Germany.

In the aftermath of war
- A democracy in distress
- 700,000 dead, $15 billion debt
- Denied territories promised by the Allies
- Militant nationalists seized Fiume

Problems
- Split between the industrial north and agrarian south
- Conflict over land, wages, and local power
- Government corruption and indecision
- Inflation, unemployment, and strikes
- Political radicalization
- Socialists won a third of seats in Chamber of Deputies
- Socialists and anarchists seized factories and farmland
- Radicals provoked a reaction from the right

The rise of Mussolini (1883–1945)
- Editor of Avantia (leading socialist daily)
- Lost editorship when he urged Italy to side with the Allies during World War I
- Founded Il Popolo d'Italia
- The Fasci
- Organized in 1914 to drum up support for the war
- Attracted young, idealist, fanatical nationalists
- The Fascist platform (1919): universal suffrage, eight-hour day, inheritance tax
- Fascist support

- Gained respect of middle classes and landowners
- Repressed radical movements of workers and peasants, attacked socialists
- Gained control of government
- 50,000 fascist militia (Black Shirts) marched on Rome, October 28, 1922
- Victor Emmanuel III invited Mussolini to form a cabinet

Italy under Mussolini
- Three components of Italian fascism
- Statism—"nothing above, outside, or against the state"
- Nationalism—the "highest form of society"
- Militarism—the "ennoblement" of man in war
- Changed the electoral laws and abolished cabinet system
- Mussolini assumed role of prime minister and party leader (duce)
- Repression and censorship
- Mussolini preached the end of class conflict
- Economy managed by 22 corporations
- More of a corrupt bureaucracy than a revolutionary economy
- Settled long conflict with Catholic Church
- Granted independence to papal residence in Vatican City
- Established Roman Catholicism as the state religion
- Maintained the capitalist status quo and "made the trains run on time"
- Offered a feeling of political involvement with no political rights

WEIMAR GERMANY
- November 9, 1918: Revolution
- Bloodless overthrow of the imperial government— Kaiser abdicated
- Social Democratic Party (SPD) announced a new German republic

- Socialists wanted democratic reforms within existing imperial bureaucracy
  Problems
- Elections not held until January 1919
- Communists and independent socialists staged armed uprisings in Berlin
- Social Democrats tried to crush the uprisings
- The martyrdom of Rosa Luxemburg and Karl Liebknecht
- The *Freikorps*
- Former army officers fighting Bolsheviks, Poles, and communists
- Fiercely right-wing anti-Marxist, anti-Semitic, and anti-liberal
  The Weimar Republic
- Coalition of Socialists, Catholic centrists, and liberal democrats
- Parliamentary liberalism (pluralism, universal suffrage, civil liberties)

The failure of Weimar
- The humiliation of World War I
- Myth that Germany was "stabbed in the back" by socialists and Jews
- What was needed was authoritarian leadership
- Versailles and reparations
- Germany lost 10% of territory
- Army reduced to 100,000
- $33 billion debt
- The Dawes Plan (1924), a new schedule of payments
- The government continued to print money
- By October 1923, a pound of potatoes cost 40 million marks
- Middle-class employees, farmers, and workers hit hardest by inflation
- Economic recovery (1925)
- Scaled-down reparation payments
- Government-sponsored building projects
- Remained dependent on capital from the United States

The Great Depression
- United States' stock market crash (1929)
- Unemployment
- Production dropped by 44%
- Peasants staged mass demonstrations
- Government cut welfare benefits
- Created opportunity for the opponents of Weimar

HITLER AND NAZISM
- Nazism: a movement that stemmed from extreme nationalism and racism.
- It was led by Adolf Hitler who was the son of an Austrian customs official.
- He dropped out of high school at age 16 aspired to be an artist and went to Vienna where he found the beliefs that shaped his life.
- The outbreak of World War I as his liberation.
- Vienna provided Hitler with extreme nationalism; Austro-Germans believed Germans were superior people and fundamental to Europe's natural rulers.
- Austro-Germans nationalists wanted to be unified with Germany and violent removal of "inferior" peoples to maintain the Austro-Hungarian Empire's power.
- Vienna's Mayor, Karl Lueger (1844-1910) impressed Hitler. Hitler absorbed anti-Semitism, racism, and hatred toward Slavs.
- Hitler developed a distorted understanding of Darwinian survival theory, the superiority of Germanic races, and the certainty of racial conflict.
- Hitler explained everything with anti-Semitism and racism.
- Hitler claimed the Jews orchestrated an international conspiracy of finance capitalism and Marxian socialism against German culture, unity, and race.
- In late 1919, Hitler joined an extremist group in Munich – the German Workers' Party, that promised German "national socialism" to eliminate capitalism's injustices and create a "people's community."

- 1921, Hitler secured complete control of the Party; he used mass rallies to push propaganda.
- 1923, the Weimar Republic was close to collapse, Hitler led an attempted armed uprising Munich.
- It was unsuccessful and Hitler was arrested.
- While in prison briefly, Hitler wrote Mein Kampf in which he outlined and developed his ideas on: race, stressing anti-Semitism; living space, broad image of war and conquered territory; and the leader-dictator, called the Fuhrer, with total power.
- Between 1924 and 1929, Hitler focused on creating and expanding his National Socialist German Workers' Party or Nazi Party.
- The Nazis were a small group until the 1929 Great Depression destroyed economic success and provided Hitler with a great opportunity.
- In 1932, 43% of the workforce was unemployed.
- Hitler made promises of economic, political, international recovery.
- Hitler rejected free-market capitalism and supported government programs to bring recovery.
- In his speeches, he aimed for middle and low-middle-class groups, and skilled workers.
- Hitler and Nazis appealed to German youth; by 1931, close to 40% of the Party were under age 30.
- In 1932, the Nazi Party became the largest party in Reichstag (German Parliament).
- German economic failure convinced people that the republican leadership was incompetent and corrupt. This increased Hitler's influence.
- 1932, Hitler won the support of major people in business and the army who thought they could use Hitler to their advantage.
- January 1933, President Paul von Hindenburg appointed Hitler, leader of Germany's largest party, Chancellor of Germany.
- Von Hindenburg hoped this would enable a conservative coalition
- February 27, 1933: Reichstag set on fire by Dutch anarchist

- Hitler suspended civil rights
- March 5, 1933: new elections
- Hitler was granted unlimited power for four years, proclaimed the Third Reich

PATH TO WAR
- Hitler set out on building a totalitarian state and expanding throughout Europe, a New Order (based on racial imperialism that favored Nordic peoples).
- In 1933, Germany withdrew from the League of Nations which was an indication of plans to rearm.
- England and France did little. Britain adopted a policy of appeasement, giving Hitler everything he wanted to avoid war.
- March 1936, Hitler sent his armies into the Rhineland, a direct violation of the Treaty of Versailles. France would not move until Britain decided to, but Britain did not.
- In 1936, Italy and Germany signed an agreement, the Rome-Berlin Axis.
- Japan wanted support for its occupation of Manchuria, and joined the Axis alliance.
- In late 1937, Hitler went forward with his plans to invade Austria and Czechoslovakia.
- When he threatened to invade Austria, Hitler forced the Austrian Chancellor in March 1938 to put local Nazis in government control. The next day, Germany moved into Austria, which became 2 provinces of Greater Germany.
- Hitler demanded the pro-Nazi, German speaking minority in western Czechoslovakia, the Sudetenland, be turned over to Germany.
- The democratic Czechoslovakia was prepared to defend itself. France and the Soviet Union were prepared to come to Czechoslovakia's aid.
- Hitler's armies occupied Czechoslovakia in March 1939.
- Hitler planned to attack Poland next. Prime Minister Neville Chamberlain declared that Britain and France would fight if Hitler attacked Poland.

- Hitler offered and Stalin signed a 10 year Nazi-Soviet nonaggression pact in August 1939.
- The pact was a promise for each country to remain neutral if the other became involved in war.
- September 1, 1939, German armies and war planes attacked Poland.
- September 3, 1939, Britain and France declared war on Germany. World War II began.

"THE FINAL SOLUTION"
- Hitler envisioned an eastern colonial empire where Poles, Ukrainians, and Russians would be enslaved and forced to die out, while Germanic peoples would resettled in these areas.
- Attempted extermination of all European Jews by the Nazi state.
- It is an example of *genocide* at its height, most extreme and hideous.
- Genocide: the deliberate and systematic destruction, partially or completely, of an ethnic, "racial," religious, or national group. It takes a few forms: actual murder or forced migration.
- Jews were not the only targets of the Nazi state, "Gypsies," Slavs, Poles, Jehovah's Witnesses, homosexuals, developmentally challenged people were included on the list of inferior people.
- After the fall of Warsaw, Nazis began deporting all German Jews to occupied Poland.
- In 1941, expulsion turned into extermination on the Russian border.
- Jews were arrested, loaded onto freight trains, and sent to extermination camps.
- January 1942 → Wansee Conference
- Berlin, Germany → leaders of the German SS (Nazi Organization) met to plan the "Final Solution."
- Those in attendance were the most fanatical and would be the ones in charge of running the death camps.
- They had mathematical sheets of data on the number of Jews in Germany and neighboring countries. The

"large" of number of Jews was a problem that had to be solved → the Final Solution.

- Lied to people and said they were going to work in factories, etc.
- Gassing people → told people they needed to shower. They were locked in shower area, an SS officer poured gas pellets in → choked to death on the poison gas agonizing, torturous death.
- This gas was invented by a Jewish Chemist → used in agriculture
- Firing squad → demanding people strip, stand close to pit and machine gun them. Anyone still moving shot in the head.
- Starvation & worked to death
- Scientific experimentation
- Bodies were checked for gold teeth, then cremated or boiled for oil to make soap.
- Ordinary Germans had little knowledge of what was happening, but recently it was revealed that there was a much broader participation of Germans in the Holocaust ← indifference to Jews' fate.
- Lesson of this event → when someone says they want to kill, believe them!
- 6 million people were killed, but some estimates are close to 11 million.
- The Holocaust, as part of World War II, was the product of a "bad mix."
- Technology + Industrial Power + Ideology+ Will Power = World War II (classmate Dr. David Hertzberg made this statement when he was a guest lecturer in my Emergence of Global Society course at St John's University in 2011).

GLOBAL CONFLICT (AS PRESENTED IN INTERNATIONAL RELATIONS/WORLD POLITICS)

CONFLICT

- The term conflict refers to armed conflict.
- Conflict is a situation against which countries negotiate.

- Countries develop capabilities that give them influence to get more favorable results than they would obtain otherwise.
- 12 wars took place in 2010; the largest are in Iraq, western Sudan (Darfur), and Afghanistan (the global South).

TYPES OF CONFLICT
- Hegemonic war: a war over control of the whole world order.
- Also known as *world war, global war, general war* or *systemic war*. (last hegemonic war was World War II)
- Total war: warfare by 1 state waged to conquer and occupy another.
- The goal is to reach the capital and force the government to surrender.
- Total war → 20th century was the century where there were numerous wars of, by, and against entire populations.
- Limited war: military actions carried out to gain some objective short of surrender and occupation of the enemy. (U.S. led war against Iraq 1991 to retake Kuwait).
- Civil war: a war between factions within a state trying to create, or prevent, a new government for the entire state or some territorial part of it.
- Guerilla war: includes certain kinds of civil wars, is warfare without front lines.
- Irregular forces operate in the midst of, and often hidden or protected by, civilian populations.
- The purpose is to harass and punish the enemy army to gradually limit its operation and effectively liberate territory from its control.
- Interstate (between states) war: 2 or more recognized independent countries against one another. (World War I & II)
- Extra-state war: war where one side is a non-state entity→ independence wars.
- Intrastate (within a state) war (civil war): fought among groups within a state/country.

WORLD WARS

- I August 1914- November 1918
- Austria-Hungary, Serbia, Germany, Russia, Bulgaria, Ottoman Empire, Italy.
- 22 million dead.
- II September 1939- September 1945
- Germany, Russia, Italy, Britain, France, U.S., Japan.
- 50 million dead, majority were civilians.

COLD WAR

- 1945-1991
- Not an actual armed conflict.
- War/conflict of ideas on politics and economics:
- "East" communism and socialism → U.S.S.R. Camp
- "West" democracy and capitalism → U.S. Camp
- Race, or contest, to show which ideology or ideas prevail. It was also a competition for "friends" or allies.
- Impacted → science and military (arms race → who can produce the best weapons).
- March 1947, the U.S. developed the Truman Doctrine → aimed to "contain" communism.
- In June 1947, Secretary of State George C. Marshall offered Europe economic aid to help rebuild – The Marshall Plan.
- In 1949, the U.S. formed an anti-Soviet military alliance of Western governments → the North Atlantic Treaty Organization (NATO)
- In 1955, Stalin (U.S.S.R.) responded with a strengthened Warsaw Pact.

TERRORISM

- *Term 1st used in 1794 during the French Revolution --- used to describe the use of terror by governments against their own citizens.(Globalization and Terrorism: the Migration of Dreams and Nightmares, Jamal Nassar)*

- *Terrorism usually refers to acts of violence by private non-state groups to advance revolutionary political goals. (p. 389 "Our Social World" 3rd edition Jeanne H. Ballantine & Keith A. Roberts 2015)*
- Political violence that targets civilians randomly.
- Stems from the lack of power.
- Terrorism is a tactic of the weak against the strong.
- Purpose is to send a message, usually after peaceful methods have been used and appeared to have been unproductive.
- The purpose is also to deflect the "terror" that a group or person might perceive themselves to experience onto those whom appear to be responsible. (BOOMERANG)
- Is not exclusive to the Islamic world.
- Because we see this tactic being used in our time by people who claim to practice Islam, doesn't mean it is solely a Muslim thing.
2 basic motives:
- 1) struggle for power & control
- 2) acts of desperation in a power struggle
- State-sponsored terrorism: government use of terrorist groups or tactics; generally controlled by the government's intelligence agency to obtain political goals or control people.
3 phases in history of terrorism:
- 1) pre-modern
- 2) early modern
- 3) current

Pre-modern → ancient times -18th century (1700s)
- Terrorism = assassinations/murders justified on ground that the person was guilty of wrongdoing. Modern day terrorism doesn't have this justification.
- Examples: early imperialist campaigns; Alexander the Great's conquest, Punic Wars (Rome & Carthage); Ottoman Turks 1456 Constantinople conquest.
- Julius Caesar's (born 100 BCE) 44BCE assassination by 60 Senators, accusation tried to make Rome a monarchy.

Early modern → 19th century – 1914

- 1881 Assassination of Tsar Alexander I who wanted reforms for Russia → industrialization & parliamentary government but was killed by anarchists 1) fight against Westernizers; 2) keep Russian institutions & tsar system.
- 1914 Archduke Franz Ferdinand in Sarajevo June.
- Imperialism in Asia (Opium Wars) & Africa (Leopold & Congo); German murder of Herero & Nama peoples in southwestern Africa. (millions killed)

Modern → WWI – present

- 1960s terrorism → global occurrence 1) more commercial air travel; 2) more TV news coverage
- Zionist movement → Palestine to create independent Jewish state.
- Holocaust Nazi regime in Germany
- USA bombings in Japan 1945 Hiroshima (Aug 6) Nagasaki (Aug 9) 1945(70,000 killed)
- Stalin's murder of 7-10 million Ukrainians; 20-25 million in Soviet Union (pogroms) "The Forgotten Genocide"
- Cold War deaths in Vietnam, Laos, Cambodia chemical warfare
- Indonesia late 1965-early 1996 genocide made possible by the U.S. military & economic support for the corrupt Suharto dictatorship.
- CIA support for Suharto's (30 yr. presidency 1967-1998) overthrow of President Ahmed Sukarno.
- Destruction of Indonesian Communist Party (PKI) 200,000 people murdered – other estimates up to 500,000.
- Cambodia 1975-1978 Communist Khmer Rouge regime under Pol Pot genocide.
- East Timor, Indonesian orchestrated genocide (U.S. U.K. Australian support) during the 1975-1999 occupation. Tortured, starved, murdered 90,800 – 202,600 includes 17,600 -19,600 violent deaths &disappearances. 2002 independence after 1999 vote for it.

- Soviet invasion of Afghanistan 1979
- 1994 Rwanda genocide 800,000 people murdered, no response from the global community.
- 2001 US Sept 11 attacks 3,000 people killed from 68 countries.
- 2003 Darfur, Sudan (Darfur is in the western part of Sudan) 2 rebel movements Sudanese Liberation Army (SLA) & Justice & Equality Movement (JEM) fought against the Sudanese government claiming they were left marginalized & unprotected from nomad attacks.
- Sudanese government sent Arab militias – the Janjaweed (devils on horseback) to attack hundreds of villages in the region.
- 400,000 killed 2,700,000 displaced.
- March 2009 President Omar al Bashir indicted by the ICC for directing mass killing, rape, & pillage against civilians.
- ICC issues arrest warrants for former Minister of State for the Interior Ahmad Harun & Ali Kushayb, Janjaweed militia leader. The government hasn't handed over either man.
- www.unitedhumanrights.org/genocide/genocide-in-sudan.htm
- 2011- present Syria
- Charles Taylor (Liberia) trial ICC 6 yrs. Gbagbo & Blé Goudé (Ivory Coast) January 2016 trial.

GLOBAL COOPERATION: GLOBAL AND REGIONAL ORGANIZATIONS

This theme/topic was covered in World History and World Politics.

CONCEPTS

Globalization
- Movement of people, goods, and services across the world.

- Speed increasingly faster as technological developments occur.

Transnational
- Between or beyond borders, includes movement of people and goods.

International
- Activity or participation by several nations across the world.

Trade
- Exchange of goods and services between and among nations.

Non-governmental Organization (NGO)
- Organization established by private organizations or people without government connection.

Multinational Corporation (MNC)
- Corporation or company with facilities and assets in at least one country other than its home country.
- The largest MNCs are (1) cars, (2) oil & (3) electronics industries.
- Financial corps essential → move $1.5 trillion daily globally.

UN, WB, IMF, WTO, WHO

UNITED NATIONS
- www.un.org
- Created October 1945 after the League of Nations proved unsuccessful in preventing the outbreak of a second major war.
- Initially 51 members, now 193 member states.
- Headquarters are in New York, NY.

- MISSION – prevention of war and maintenance of peace and security.
- Roles have been expanded since 1945 to include:
- Human Rights recognition
- Relief efforts
- Development projects
  UN –Main Bodies:
  General Assembly (192 member states)
- Policymaking and representative body of the UN.
  Security Council (5 permanent members, 10 non-permanent members)
- Has the primary responsibility for maintaining international peace and security.
  Secretariat
- Carries out day-to-day work of the UN.
  Economic and Social Council (54 members)
- Coordinates economic, social, and other related work for the UN.
  Trusteeship Council
- Provided supervision of 11 Trust Territories that by 1994, have achieved independence.

International Court of Justice (15 judges)
- Settles disputes between states and gives advisory opinions to UN and its agencies.

WORLD BANK
- www.worldbank.org
- The World Bank is made up of two institutions the IBRD and the International Development Association (IDA).
- Headquarters are in Washington D.C.
- International Bank for Reconstruction and Development (IBRD) was the original name of the World Bank, which was established 1944 to assist European nations devastated by World War II to rebuild.

- The WB has extended its function to (1) promoting globalization and (2) contributing to the development of nations by providing financial and technical assistance.

INTERNATIONAL MONETARY FUND

- www.imf.org
- In 1944 at a meeting of 45 nations in Bretton Woods, New Hampshire, the IMF was proposed, today it is made up of 190 nations.
- Headquarters are in Washington D.C.
- They intended to prevent another economic breakdown like the Great Depression.
- The IMF came into full effect 1945 with 29 governments.
- MISSION → (1) encourage financial cooperation globally, (2) provide financial security, (3) aid in international trade, (4) support economic growth, and (5) reduce poverty.

WORLD HEALTH ORGANIZATION

- www.who.int/en
- Part of the UN and became active 1948.
- WHO has responsibility for
- (1) health concerns
- (2) outlining global health research agenda
- (3) setting health standards
- (4) providing technical support to countries
- (5) supervising and reviewing health developments

WORLD TRADE ORGANIZATION

- www.wto.org
- Originally, the General Agreement on Tariffs and Trade (GATT) created 1949, but became the WTO 1995.
- The WTO has 150 members and deals with trade terms and agreements among nations.
- Headquarters Geneva, Switzerland.

- It aims to ensure trade flows are smooth and free.
- Nations negotiate and their parliaments approve trade agreements.

OAS, AL, EU, AU, ASEAN, MERCOSUR

ORGANIZATION OF AMERICAN STATES (OAS)
- www.oas.org/en
- The OAS began in 1826 when Simón Bolívar convened the Congress of Panama.
- The OAS did not meet regularly until after 1889 in Washington D.C., at the First International Conference of American States.
- Made up of 35 states.
- Headquarters in Washington D.C.
- Purpose to (1) resolve disagreements & disputes among member states, (2) promote democracy & human rights, (3) improve business & commercial relations.

ARAB LEAGUE (AL)
- www.arableagueonline.org
- Founded in 1945 in Cairo, Egypt which is also the organization's headquarters.
- There are 22 members today.
- Purpose of the League of Arab States is to (1) strengthen ties among member states, (2) coordinate policies, and (3) promote their common interests.

EUROPEAN UNION (EU)
- http://europa.eu
- There are 27 member nations.
- An economic-political organization of European nations aimed to end conflict.

- Began as the European Coal and Steel Community (ECSC) in 1950 to unite European countries in an effort to keep peace.
- Belgium, France, Luxemburg, Italy, the Netherlands, and Germany were the original 6 members.
- In 1957, Treaty of Rome established the European Economic Community (EEC) or "Common Market".
- In 1993, Treaty of Maastricht established the European Union.

AFRICAN UNION (AU)
- www.african-union.org
- Began as the Organization for African Unity (OAU) in 1963, which aimed to (1) purge colonialism from the continent, (2) promote unity among African states, (3) coordinate cooperation for development, and (4) protect the sovereignty of new states.
- There are 55 member states.
- Headquarters in Addis Ababa, Ethiopia.
- In 1999, Heads of State & Government of the OAU issued a Declaration to create an African Union to speed the process of integration in the African continent, to allow it to play its role in the global economy.
- AU intended to handle numerous issues: social, economic, and political that have been further complicated by globalization's negative aspects.

ASSOCIATION OF SOUTHEAST ASIAN NATIONS (ASEAN)
- www.aseansec.org
- Created 1967 in Bangkok, Thailand by Indonesia, Malaysia, Philippines, Singapore, and Thailand.
- There are now 10 member states with headquarters in Jakarta, Indonesia.

- Goals are to (1) accelerate economic growth, (2) social progress & cultural development, and (3) promote peace & security in the region.

MERCOSUR
- www.mercosur.int/
- Argentina, Brazil, Paraguay, & Uruguay signed the Treaty of Asuncion in 1991, to establish the Southern Common Market, Mercosur.
- The 4 member states of Mercosur share values expressed in their support of democratic, pluralistic societies that promote basic freedoms.
- It also upholds human rights & the protection of environmental & sustainable development.
- It is committed to strengthening democracy, legal security, poverty alleviation, economic development, and social equity.
- The main goal of members is to integrate through:

  o free movement of goods, services, & tools of production
  o creation of a Common External Tariff (CET)
  o adoption of a common commercial policy
  o coordination of macroeconomic polices
  o blended legalization in relevant areas

African societies, states, and economic activities. I present highlights of the basic structures and characteristics of traditional African communities around the 1500s for both Modern African history and African-American history. Over time for African History I decided which communities I wanted to feature to provide a diversity of traditional practices and chose specific facts to present to students to give them a general picture of traditional Africa. These facts are noted by the bullet points.

WEST AFRICA

I.   HAUSA STATES

Modern day northern Nigeria

- Traditions of Hausa states in northern Nigeria go back to the kings of the 11th century.

  - The *Kano Chronicle,* a collection of Hausa traditions recorded centuries later, says that the first king or *Sarki* of Kano was Bogoda, who came to power in 999.

  - Other Hausa communities transitioned into states with kings at the end of the 13th century.

- Hausa state had three key reasons for existence:

- *A place of government and military defense.*

- Neighboring farmers could seek refuge when threatened by raiders. They paid taxes to the ruling men of the city in exchange for protection.

- *A market-place for the nearby countryside.*

- This is where they were able to exchange their products for goods that town craftsmen made, like leather.

- *A center for long-distance trade.*

- They became a center for trade in products from North Africa, Egypt, the rest of the Sudan, and Guinea.

To increase strength and wealth, the cities had to become powerful, this power had to extend to the countryside, which was difficult to accomplish.

- There is the story of Sarki Shekkarau in 1290, to which delegates reported "disloyalty" among the country people who wanted to keep their customs and beliefs.

  - Shekkarau allowed them to keep their customs.

  - This is where they applied diplomacy to come to an agreement that would benefit both the cities and countryside.

- There are five (5) Hausa cities that were involved in trade and politics → Daura, Gobir, Katsina, Kano, & Zaria.

- There was both cooperation and rivalry among them.

- The Hausa states never formed a central government or empire, but there were Muslim governmental methods applied.

- They did interact peacefully and engaged in trade with the Yoruba and other neighboring peoples.

- The Hausa were known for their strengths in farming and trade; their states became a strong and stable part of West Africa.

- Power was shared between the people of noble and ordinary families.

- Kings gave some of their power to people of ordinary families, 'commoners' or the 'king's men' to decrease the nobles' power.

- A form of 'constitutional monarchy' or limited rule developed.

- The king was able to act in important matters only with the agreement of senior chiefs and officials.

- There was also a 'checks and balances' system.

SENEGAMBIA

II.   JOLOF EMPIRE

Modern day Senegal

- Soon after 1300, the Wolof people founded the small state of Jolof in the central part of Senegal.

- The Jolof was ruled by a king, *Burba*, through ruling families. (As adopted by the Soninke of Ghana and Mandinka of Mali).

- Descent-line chiefs had religious duties as leaders of ceremonies by which one people linked themselves with their "founding ancestors" in the world of spirits.

- The *Burba* Jolof had religious and political power over smaller Wolof states Cayor, Walo, and Baol.

- The Burba and his government of Jolof joined these small states into a powerful Wolof Empire during the 15th century.

At the same time, a related people, the Serer, formed a state called Sine-Salum that became an outlying part of the Wolof Empire.

- Jolof government was aristocratic.

  - It was ruled by privileged men or nobles who drew their power from being born into ruling families.

  - Political strength came from their leadership in (1) warfare, (2) control of trade, and (3) close alliance with one another under the rule of the *Burba.*

- They also had religious power, stemming from Wolof beliefs about the spiritual character of their rulers.

- Most people had no political rights of much value; they had to serve lineage chiefs, pay tribute in cattle & other goods, and work for lineage chiefs when required.

- There was a gradual decrease in Wolof power after the development of European sea-trade along the coast of Senegal.

- European contacts began in the 1440s, Portuguese sailors & soldiers built up a presence on the little island of Arguin, north coast of Mauretania.

- They raided the mainland for captives whom they took back to Portugal and sold into slavery.

- In the 1450s there was a partnership between the *Burba* Jolof, his subject kings, and the Portuguese.

  - They were willing to sell captives to buy European goods like metal ware, cotton, cloth and weapons.

  - This trade partnership led to a political alliance with the Portuguese.

- The states of Jolof were able to maintain their independence until the late 19th century when the French invaded. They had formed a notable part of West African civilization.

Around 1400 the Susu people formed a state called the Futa Jallon that lied in the center of modern republic of Guinea. Other Susu moved down to the coast where their descendants now live, while a branch of the Fulani won control of Futa Jallon, remaining there to this day.

In Sierra Leone, new states began to be formed by the migrating Bulom, Temne, and Mende peoples on both sides of the Scarcies River.

Revolutionary changes occurred when European ships sailed in from Portugal, Spain, England, and France bringing firearms and new forms of warfare, and the beginnings of the slave trade.

FOREST KINGDOMS: THE DELTA OF THE NIGER

Toward the end of the 15th century, the Portuguese found powerful kingdom of Benin in the bight (wide bay) of Benin. Curiosity about Portugal led the King of Benin to send one of his chiefs as an ambassador to Lisbon.

Benin had other kingdoms in its neighborhood and other countries that had states but were decentralized without a king.

These kingdoms belonged to what can be called the "Yoruba group" and the "government without rulers" to the "Igbo group."

III.   OYO EMPIRE OF THE YORUBA

Modern day southwestern Nigeria

- West of the kingdom of Benin is the home of the Yoruba who took shape several thousand years ago.

- One tradition says that their origin was at Ile-Ife, an ancient town in Yorubaland that mankind was created.

- Another tradition tells the story of Oduduwa, a great ancestor who settled at Ile-Ife and sent out his descendants to rule the branches of the Yoruba.

Archaeological evidence indicates the Yoruba were pioneering metalworkers and fine artists in baked clay and possibly related to the people of the Nok culture.

To determine the source of the ancestors personified in Oduduwa who would build the Yoruba civilization, linguistics have given evidence through language patterns that suggests there were possibly two main movements of incoming ancestors, one towards Ekiti, Ife, and Ijebu in the tropical forest, and the other towards Oyo. The earliest of these migrations probably started soon after 700.

Some Yoruba legends say that their ancestors came from Arabia, some of their customs reflecting the ideas of peoples from ancient Kush. There is no doubt that these ancestors came from the Western Sudan, possibly a little way north of Yorubaland, where they had been influenced by the Nile civilizations that sent out traders and travelers in ancient times.

- The Yoruba relied on forest farming and their political life was controlled by town government and not village government.

- The Yoruba had skills of neighboring peoples like farming, iron-smelting, cotton-weaving, and other handicrafts.

- Their principal contribution to West African civilization was their urban centers.

- During ancient times, the capital towns of Yoruba states were linked together in a confederation under the spiritual and political leadership of the senior Yoruba ruler, the *Oni* of Ife, and by arrangements between ruling families.

- This system allowed each state to run its own affairs and promoted peace.

- With the rise of Oyo in northern Yorubaland during the 16th century, the central influence of Ife declined.

- The Yoruba used the *Ebi* system, under which the kingdom was seen as a larger version of a family & a collection of kingdoms' rulers viewed one another as relations.

Seniority was based on believed ages of the different kingdoms. The Oyo Empire cut across arrangements by claiming the leadership of a 'junior' kingdom, this left the Oyo Empire and Ebi system in conflict.

The capitals were organized in a way that combined segmentary patterns of authority with government by ruling families and *obas* (kings).

- Ife reached the height of its artistic and political achievement soon after 1300.

- Oyo were not only traders, but skilled in cloth production – spinning, dyeing, weaving cotton.

- By the 17th century Oyo empire was large. Under the supreme leader or *Alafin* grew in influence.

- Alafin Abiodun (1770-1789) began intense policies of economic development especially of the trade of slaves with Europeans along the coast.

- The Alafin's power was limited in the 18th century.

  - There was a council of senior 'big family' nobles, the Oyo Mesi, under the leader the *Bashorun*.

  - The entire system was based on a balance between the Alafin and his 'king's men' or appointed officials, on one side, and the Oyo Mesi and other nobles on the other.

  - The power of the Oyo Mesi had the right to declare an Alafin had lost the confidence of the ancestors and had to commit suicide, they could then choose another Alafin.

  - There was another 'built in' balance – the chiefs of the Ogboni Association. They could revoke the Oyo Mesi's decision to remove an Alafin.

The Alafin faced troubles as a result of the growth of the coastal trade in slaves and firearms that helped to spread warfare and raiding.

NIGER DELTA PEOPLES

IV.   IGBO

Modern day southeastern Nigeria

- The history of the Delta people began in the 16th century; their ancestors probably came from the area of Benin and Iboland.

  - Population pressure and new coastal trade with European sea-merchants brought more people to the delta lands.

  - These people were of several origins: *Ijo, Igbo, Edo, Jekri, Ibibio, Efik,* and some *Tiv* and *Fulani* from the north.

These people were also called *Ndu Mili Nnu*, People of the Salt Water, by the inland Igbo. They dominated the trade of the whole Niger Delta from the Cross River to the River of Benin; they also opened up routes of sea trade to the Igbo of the inland.

- Their political organization was fragmented; there was no central ruler or government.

- Local people would unite to form a 'city-state' for trade reasons, but governed itself and its surrounding villages only.

- There were several states in the Delta of this type around the middle of the 17th century.

- There were city-states ruled by kings, Ibani, New Calabar (Kalabari), and Warri elected by members of their wealthiest and most prominent families.

Among the republics were Brass and the market towns of Old Calabar in the Cross River (Creek Town, Henshaw Town, Duke Town, and Obutong); they were ruled as republics by members of special political associations.

- The day-to-day life of people was organized through a *House System*, a new development that replaced the traditional way of rule by clans of big families.

- The House was a type of co-operative trading company based on the commercial association between the Head of the House, his family, his trading assistants and his servants.

- The full development of these Houses did not occur until after 1800.

- Igbo have lived in the region east of the lower part of the Niger since early human history.

- Historically, the Igbo were always divided into five large groups differing somewhat in language, customs, ways of work, and religion.

- All Igbo societies had skilled craftsmen in weaving, metal-working and other activities like local trade. They practiced forest agriculture.

- There were different types of Igbo government.

  - Most Igbo have governed themselves without giving power to chiefs (decentralized- not centered in one person or group).

  - Some like the Nri Awka near the Niger, had kings; the people of the eastern Delta used political associations.

Almost all Igbo divided themselves into 'age-sets' each of which had their own special rights, duties, and responsibilities.

- Igbo village governments were popular.

- Every adult man, and women in some cases, had a say at village assemblies where common interests were handled.

- These types of government fostered individual development.

- Promotion within the village government was by achievement, not credit.

- Village governments were in line with the democratic habits of the modern world.

V.   DAHOMEY KINGDOM

Modern day Benin

- Dahomey was a subject area of the Oyo Empire.

- During the 17th century several small states existed on the coast and in the interior which included Whydah, Jakin, Grand Popo, and Great Andrah.

- They took advantage of the sea trade including the slave trade.

- Local rulers set prices, levied taxes, and controlled bargaining with the Europeans.

  - As the demand for slaves increased, the coastal states extended their raids deeper into the interior.

  - This caused friction with the inland Fon people.

- The Fon organized themselves around successful military leaders.

- Their state emerged from the town of Abomey around 1650.

- Men and women participated in military service.

- Under King Agaja, who ruled for 30 years (circa 1710 -1740), Abomey captured the coastal states.

  - King Agaja was determined to stop the slave raids and export of slaves which served as the major motivation in forming the state.

  - As the Fon began to unify themselves they had a greater need for firearms and gun powder.

- By the middle of the 18th century, Dahomey had established control along the coast.

- Whydah became the subject to Fon authority which was represented by Dahomean officials, including one to supervise trade with Europeans.

- Special permission was necessary for a European to visit Abomey, but near the end of the 18th century, there seems to have been a regular flow of Europeans between the coast and capital.

- This is one sign of Dahomey's increased reliance on the slave trade.

- Given the competition for firearms and other items from Europeans the slave trade became a logical venture for Dahomey.

The Alafin of Oyo defeated Agaja's forces in 1726 and launched other attacks to stop Dahomey's growing power. Dahomey became more involved in the slave trade to get more guns and powder and owed its rise and greatness to the slave trade's profits.

- Dahomey was one of the few absolute monarchies in the region.

  - The king did have an advisory council, but he appointed and dismissed all state officials.

  - Top officials included a (1) police chief, (2) tax collector, (3) minister of agriculture, and (4) army commander.

  - The state was divided into six districts each supervised by an administrator.

  - Parallel to the state officials was a group of women, called the king's wives, who were assigned to oversee the work of a particular official. Each woman appointed workers to check on reports of her assigned official.

- Dahomey had unique system that gave women a very crucial role in political affairs.

The country's national symbol was the perforated calabash filled with water and each citizen symbolically held a finger in a perforation to prevent loss of water. Foreigners could become citizens by actually placing a finger in the hole of a calabash during a symbolic citizenship ceremony.

- Dahomey reached the peak of its power 1790- 1850. In 1818 King Gezo declared independence from the Oyo Empire.

- After the slave trade, Dahomey shifted focus on ivory and palm oil until the era of colonialism.

VI.   ASHANTI KINGDOM

   Modern day Ghana and Ivory Coast

- Sometime during the 12th or 13th century it seems the ancestors of the Akan people migrated to the regions of modern Ghana and Ivory Coast.

   - They established control over the gold-producing area and maintained commercial contacts with the Western Sudan.

   - They took advantage of the coastal trade especially after the arrival of Europeans.

- Several small states emerged: Bon, Adansi, Denkyera, Akwamu, and others.

- Denkyera and Akwamu were the most powerful during the 17th century.

- Denkyera expanded westward with its ally Akim and Akwamu expanded eastward with its ally Ashanti.

Akwamu's armies early in the 18th century occupied Whydah across the Volta River, bringing the Ewe and Ho areas under its authority.

- By 1710 Ashanti began asserting its power, simultaneously, the Fon were extending their control over the coastal city-states of Dahomey, and the Fante were emerging from Akwamu dominance.

- Ashanti dominated the commercial and political scene of the region for 200 years.

- Kumasi is the capital of Ashanti (now a region in modern day Ghana); it was a commercial center as well as meeting place for political and religious leaders.

- Traditions say that Asantehene Osei Tutu and his adviser and priest, Okomfo Anokye, were the founders of the Ashanti nation around 1695.

- Anokye declared that the Akan supreme God, Nyame, instructed him to make Ashanti a great power.

- At a mass assembly called by Osei Tutu, Anokye caused a golden stool to appear from the sky and rest on Osei Tutu's knees.

- This stool was then described as containing the collective soul of the Ashanti people.

Osei Tutu was able to establish unity by forbidding people to speak of former separate traditions.

- During the 1690s, the most powerful state, Denkyera, secured European goods like guns and ammunition through its control of the coastal trade.

- They provided the Europeans with gold and slaves, usually Ashanti people.

- Denkyera was defeated shortly after 1700 and Ashanti extended its dominance over the region.

- Kumasi became a center for merchants, teachers, and politicians.

Southward movement of the Ashanti put them into direct contact with the Europeans where they developed a commercial partnership with the Dutch at Elmina.

The coastal people, the Fante, were uniting the area between Elmina and Accra; they developed a trading partnership with the British at Cape Coast.

Competition between the Fante and Ashanti led to the war of 1806 where the Ashanti were victorious. For the rest of the 19th century, British presence and power on the coast increased as well as their support of the Fante which increased friction with the Ashanti.

The Dutch left the coast in 1872, leaving the British.

CENTRAL AFRICA

I.   THE KONGO KINGDOM
     Modern day Angola, Republic of the Congo, and Democratic Republic of the Congo

- The kingdom of Kongo was probably founded in the 14th century.
  - It had a hierarchical structure from the basic unit of the village under a headman.
  - Several villages combined to form a district under an official.
  - A province was made up of several districts under an official.
  - At the center of the kingdom was the king or Manikongo who appointed and removed all officials.

- The king was selected by a council of elders who chose the most popular candidate from one of the two dynastic families.

- The kingdom had a high degree of centralization.
  - The king maintained a royal fishery that provided shells as a medium of exchange.

- The king had a well-armed guard, but no standing army.

- The Portuguese explorer Diogo Cao found this kingdom at the mouth of the Kongo River in 1482.
    - In 1485, he brought four Portuguese missionaries with him to the Kongo and took four Congolese to Portugal.
    - He persuaded the king to send an ambassador to Lisbon to request assistance, technicians, and missionaries.

- Several Congolese were sent to Portugal for education.

- In 1491, Portuguese missionaries, artisans, and explorers arrived and began a program of foreign aid to the African kingdom.
    - A Portuguese community emerged under the authority of the Congolese king.
    - They built churches and converted Congolese to Christianity.

A convert named Alphonso ascended to the throne in 1506, he attempted to create a Christian state with the support of King Manuel in Portugal.

- The Portuguese were interested in developing influence in trade and acquiring an ally against enemies.

    - Because the Portuguese in the Kongo did not respect the Congolese people, this effort failed.

    - In addition the slave trade provided an opportunity to acquire wealth.

- As the slave trade became more profitable, the Portuguese became bolder in their disregard for the Congolese.

- The Manikongo sent the Portuguese king and Pope several protests in 1526.

- Portuguese merchants had bribed and hired Congolese slave raiders and encouraged subordinate officials to rebel against the king.

- Wealth and firearms fed the slave trade which led to the decline of the kingdom and intensified animosity and war among diverse African peoples in the area.

Civil disorder spread, slave exports increased, and Portuguese invasions resulted in destruction and several deaths including King Antonio I (r. 1661-1665).

- By 1720, the Kongo kingdom barely existed.

The Portuguese defeated the Ngola people and laid the foundation for colonial rule in Angola.

II.   THE MUTAPA EMPIRE

Modern day Zambia, Zimbabwe, Mozambique

- The empire of Mutapa emerged between the Zambezi and Limpopo Rivers and centered on the stone buildings of Zimbabwe.

- These buildings are the work of the Shona people in the 14th century.

- The Shona are a Bantu group who may have migrated from the Congo during the early years of the 14th century.

- They rose to power under the kings of Rozwi/Rozvi clan from about 1420.

- King Mutota set out on a military campaign that brought large territories under his power and gave him the title of Mwene Mutapa or Master Soldier.

- By the end of the 15th century he extended his power to the Kalahari Desert and Indian Ocean.

- The East African and Asian trade brought Zimbabwe into the network where it was a key source of ivory, gold and copper.

- It had a centralized regime strengthened by the Shona belief that only the Mwene Mutapa could communicate with the spirits giving him ultimate religious authority and rule by divine right.

- Unity was symbolized by the royal fire that burned throughout the king's reign.

  - Each subordinate ruler carried a flame to his district and kept a light as a symbol of unity.
  - Each year the districts' flames were relit from the royal fire to show continued loyalty.

- When a new king ascended the throne, the royal fire was put out and a new one ignited.

- The Mwene Mutapa, his adviser, and officials pursued a policy of unification and state building, but internal rivalries retarded this along with European interference.

- This led to the disruption of the kingdom.

THE SLAVE TRADE: ORIGINS, GROWTH, END

INDIAN OCEAN SLAVE TRADE

The trade in enslaved Africans on the East coast of Africa predated the Trans-Atlantic trade by several centuries. The trade increased and expanded southward as Muslim Arabs settled along the coast from the early 8th century.

The overall volume of the trade probably was small, because gold and ivory remained key commodities even during the height of the trade in the 19th century.

The principal demand for East African slaves, prior to the 19th century, came from the Arabian Peninsula, Persia, India, and very likely China. On the Arabian Peninsula, in Persia and India, the enslaved Africans were used primarily as mercenary soldiers, domestic servants, concubines, crewmen on dhows, and dock workers. Some were also used as pearl divers in Bahrain, while the date plantations and coconut groves of Basra, the Batinah Coast, Bandar Abbas, and a few other areas along the Persian Gulf employed slaves as gang labor.

Arabs were the principal slave dealers in the Indian Ocean areas. Before the 19th century, they seldom ventured into the interior, but profited from their legitimate business contacts on the coast and purchased slaves from coastal allies, many of whom were mixed Arab African descent - the Swahili.

This peaceful trade developed alongside kidnappings and raids; an advantage Arabs had in East Africa that Europeans did not have in West Africa was a long history of trade and settlement among Africans. From the late 18th century, Arab political rule on the coast virtually assured lucrative slave traffic to Asia.

When Said ibn Sultan established authority over Zanzibar in 1806, several of his Omani compatriots migrated to the island in search of economic gain; cloves were introduced in 1818, and large plantations developed increasing the demand for cheap labor to clear the land. This development led to the expansion of the slave trade.

European and American slavers also tapped the East African supply purchasing slaves from Arab and Indian merchants.

One of the factors affecting the expansion of the slave trade in East Africa was the gradual effectiveness of the abolition of the traffic in West Africa in 1807 when Britain and the US, in 1808, legally abolished the trade. This caused many slavers to seek enslaved Africans in the East.

As European political and economic influence in North Africa amplified from the 1790s, the northern slave ports of the Trans-

Saharan and Nile Valley were gradually drawn into the European path of legitimate trade. Arab slavers shifted their activities to the Red Sea and East African coast.

From about the middle of the 18th century French settlers in the Indian Ocean colonies of Mauritius and Reunion, developed sugar and coffee plantations which relied on labor from East Africa.

East Africa during the 19th century became a major source of slaves for Asia and European settlers in the Orient.

ATLANTIC OCEAN SLAVE TRADE

- *By the early 17th century, ships from several European nations arrived on the West African coast between Senegal in the west and the Gulf of Benin in the east.*

- These Europeans competed with one another, but the Portuguese led the way; w/ an advantage over the English and French.
- The Dutch came to West Africa & took the lead in trade with Africa. In 1637, the Dutch attacked and seized the Portuguese castle at Elmina. Five years later the Dutch threw the Portuguese out of the Gold Coast completely.
- Africans were aware of the rivalry among the Europeans and took sides according their own interests. European sea-merchants continued coming.
- At first a peaceful trading partnership emerged.

Of the 41 trading castles Europeans eventually built in West Africa, at least 28 were built before 1700.

The 17th century was the period of the establishment of European- American trade with West Africa, the 18th was the period of its large expansion.

- *Africans initially had the upper hand, but in the late 18th century, with growing European control of the coastal trade, the balance of power came down on the European side.*

73

- *Before, Europeans had to pay rent for land on which their trade forts were built;* Africans often attacked the forts and seized them.
- They were in control of their side of the trade, were strong enough to check Europeans, and used Europeans for their own political interests and needs.
- This relationship changed when Africans could not control what the Europeans wanted to buy from them.
- Primary thing Europeans demanded were slaves.

- *Why Africans?* → *Knowledge of tropical agriculture and immunity to diseases made them the best suited.*
- *Last to be considered among indigenous Americans and Europeans b/c they had to be captured and transported which was expensive and dangerous.*

- *The slave trade began as a large and regular trade system only after 1625.*
- *At this time the Portuguese, Spanish, French, English, Dutch, and Danes established colonies in North and South America.*

- *The major source of slaves in West Africa was Angola which was specifically the main supply base for slaves to Brazil.*
  - *This region wasn't patrolled by the West Africa Squadron, a British initiative to stop the slave trade.*
  - *Angola eventually suffered the greatest depopulation.*

Within the European colonies in the Americas more mines and plantations were opened. They wanted more and more slaves; they went to Africa to buy or capture them. They bought or captured several million Africans.

- *Why did this trade begin and grow?*
  - *Rooted in the master-servant organization that existed in many West African states & other parts of the world.*

- *Kings and chiefs turned war-captives and certain classes of law breakers into slaves, they were not very different from most other people, except they had fewer rights.*
- *They were servants who had to perform special duties and work.*
- Slavery in Africa was much less cruel servitude than the chattel slavery that developed in the Americas.

- The slave trade grew out of old customs of chiefs and kings who were accustomed to seeing all war-prisoners as property. Additionally wealth was based on labor control.
    - The lords of old West Africa bought and sold people to North Africa and Arabia as did the lords of Europe and Asia.
    - Client → someone chooses to become a dependent of another person– usually done in a time of crisis → famine, avoid death, escape catastrophe.
    - Pawn → someone given as collateral on a loan → debt repaid, person returned.

- *Europeans asked for slaves more than anything else because European settlers in the Americas wanted cheap labor more than gold or ivory.*
- *African kings, chiefs, and merchants were stuck in the trade partnership because they still wanted European products.*
    - *Kings and chiefs were willing participants because they began to need the guns that they were getting from the Europeans.*
    - *If Europeans could not buy captives at one port along the coast, they would continue on to the next market.*

The musket became the most powerful weapon of that time, chiefs and kings living in a non-industrial society could not manufacture them themselves, they had to purchase them from abroad.

The overseas slave trade that began small became a huge export of captured men and women to the Americas.

There were numerous cases of African kings and chiefs seeing how destructive this trade was to peace and prosperity at home, attempted to stop it, but the pressure proves too strong for them. Eventually the overseas slave trade spread to lands beyond the coast profiting from the disunity among African peoples.

→ *From England alone, at the height of the 18th century African trade, the gunsmiths of Birmingham provided more than 100,000 a year. By selling these guns, Europeans helped to spread war among Africans, because buying guns called for the capture of war-prisoners who could be sold into slavery. But the guns also strengthen Africans against European invasion or attack.*

CONSEQUENCES OF THE TRADE

- *After 1600, it was increasingly the European demand for slave labor that dominated the coastal markets and sent its influence far inland.*

- *The slave trade was a disaster for African peoples.*
  - *A greater portion of Africa's youth (14-35 yrs. old) was exported adversely affecting future (1) social relations, (2) reproduction, (3) labor, and (4) cultural and political leadership.*
  - *The fear induced by the slave raids/ trade created a climate not beneficial to cultural growth.*

The trade was bad in different ways in different places, yet worst for the captives. Once delivered to European and American ships, they were stripped, branded, and pushed into airless under decks, crushed together, often chained by hand and foot. They crossed the Atlantic Ocean like this for weeks; one in every six captives died on this voyage.

- *Many millions of strong young men and women were forced out of Africa by the slave trade.*
  - *Between 10 and 15 million landed alive in the Americas.*

76

- *Millions were lost in raids and wars for captives, and during the "Middle Passage" across the Atlantic.*
- *Long-term consequence of the slave trade was in terms of production and politics.*
- *In production, the slave trade obligated Africa to export its most valuable source of wealth → human labor.*
  - *In politics, the slave trade brought unnecessary wars.*

By African slave labor they created wealth and profits for America and Europe, not Africa. What Africa received in exchange was manufactured goods from Europe.

- This exchange of raw material (human labor) for manufactured goods (guns) was an early type of *colonial exchange*.
- The slave trade transformed West Africa into a subject part of the European and American economic systems.

- *The slave trade opened the way for the colonial system that would follow in the late 19th century.*
  - a. *It helped to pull West Africa back, and push Europe and America forward.*

- *Another consequence of the Atlantic trade happened outside of Africa.*
- *Large populations of African origin were taken to lands beyond the Atlantic that would play a notable role in building the civilizations of the Americas.*

RESISTANCE TO THE TRADE

There were African efforts to cut down and even stop the slave trade.

- *In 1526, King Nzinga Mbemba of the Bakongo state of Kongo wrote an angry letter to the king of Portugal complaining that the slave trade was greatly harming his country.*

  - *King Nzinga Mbemba revealed that Portuguese traders were 'grabbing and selling' his people and even members of his own family.*

77

- *He demanded the Portuguese king remove his traders from Kongo and that there should be neither trade in slaves nor any market for slaves.'*
- *The demands of the sea-merchants were too much for the king's chiefs and sub-chiefs and so the trade continued.*

- *Queen Nzinga of Ndongo in the 1620s- 1640s led armed resistance against Portuguese slavers to end the slave trade and negotiated treaties to establish her rule.*

- *King Agaja in Dahomey sent armies to capture Andrah (Allada) and other slave-dealing centers on the coast in 1724.*

- *In 1789, a Swedish traveler in northern Senegal wrote about the Alamy of the state of Futa Toro who passed a law that declared no slaves were to be taken through Futa Toro for sale abroad.'*
- *The Alamy was up against a powerful trading system too strong which defeated his good intentions."*

French slave ships were waiting in the Senegal river, but the captains saw they could not get any slaves; they complained to the Alamy against his law. *He refused to back down and revoke it; he sent back presents the French slave trading company gave him saying "all the riches of the company would not make him change his mind."* Inland slave dealers found a way to work around the Alamy's law and continued taking captives to the coast by another route.

- *Acts of resistance or attempted resistance often failed because the slave trade had become a valuable part of the commercial system of the western world until after 1800.*
- *Only a change in this system could stop the slave trade. → Creation of the free republics of Sierra Leone (1787) and Liberia (1822).*

- *Slave trade officially abolished by Britain in 1807 and the U.S. 1808, but an illegal trade continued into the 1880s.*

Total numbers of Africans to specific countries in Americas [3]

Brazil   3,902,000 or 40.7%

          Congo- Angola, Cape Verde, Guinea, Ghana, Mozambique, Tanzania.

Jamaica   1,077,100 or 11.2%

          Liberia, Ghana, Togo, Benin, western Nigeria

Cuba   (Spanish islands) 791, 900

          Republic of Congo, Angola, Mozambique, Nigeria, Cameroon, Benin

Haiti   787,400 or 8.2%

          Mali (Bambara), Eastern Nigeria, Guinea, Benin, Aradas, Yorubas, Minas, Bouriqui

U.S.   361, 100 or 3.8 %

AFRICA POST- DECOLONIZATION

POWER TRANSFER

When the British, French, and Belgians decided to give up power to their African colonies, they did so rapidly, which was indicative of problems with control. Riots in the Gold Coast 1948, the Mau rebellion in Kenya early 1950s, and the breakdown of law and order in Nyasaland (Malawi) mid-1950s showed Britain that containing nationalism would be expensive.

- For European powers the key goal was to keep as much power, especially economic control, as possible. Rapid decolonization lessened the level of conflict between colonial powers and African nationalist leaders.

---

[3] This is from an independent study paper on slavery in these countries.

- European powers moved to exclude aspects of nationalist movements seen as dangerous and help leaders and parties friendlier to European economic interests. One example was Cameroon and French elimination of the Union de Populations Camerounaises (UPC), a radical movement.

- Most nationalist leaders supported the legitimacy of private property and other capitalist principles resulting from the influence of their own class and personal goals.
  - In most countries the economic interests of European powers were largely preserved.

For 1st wave of African countries to receive independence, a final colonial rule legacy was left ---formal structures of democratic rule. British colonies received negotiated variations of the basic Westminster parliamentary government type where the prime minster is chosen from elected parliament members and where the executive and legislative powers are fused.

The French model was a president-centered form where the legislative and executive branches are separate.

The first period of decolonization roughly 1957-1969, saw more than 30 new African states obtain sovereignty.

COLONIAL IMPACT ON AFRICAN POLITICS

- The first impacts of colonialism on African politics were the superimposed artificial geographical forms and distortion of traditional social and economic patterns.
- Geographical units were developed that landlocked a few, if any, resources, or enclosed existing diverse and highly competitive cultural and political systems.
- The result was a political map that created major differences among various African countries in future

potential for nation-building, economic development, and stability.

African colonies were made subordinate to European political and economic needs.

Independence was not the result of a long process of preparation where the goal was long known and the methods carefully developed.

The democratic models developed by the French and British for their colonies were alien structures hastily superimposed over the deeply ingrained political legacies of imperial rule. The real political inheritances of African states were authoritarian colonial state structures.

- Imperial rule seized political power; the colonial powers created governing systems mostly intended to (1) control territorial populations, (2) implement natural resource exploitation, and (3) maintain themselves and the European population.

- Colonial rule was highly authoritarian and supported by police forces and colonial troops.
    - Future African leaders were exposed to authoritarian control and were used to government justified by force.
    - Ideas of authoritarianism being appropriate mode of rule were part of the colonial political legacy.

- New state politics was shaped by 4 influential societal circumstances:
- All colonial territories experienced growing inequalities between social classes.
- British model of indirect rule through social tribal rulers, heightened identification with and competition between ethnic groups.
- Postcolonial politics included drastic population shifts from rural areas to cities.
- Discriminatory colonial educational policies provided little money for access to education for most African until after WWI. African countries entered

independence ill-equipped to staff government agencies, private businesses, or development organizations.

ORGANIZATION OF AFRICAN UNITY (OAU 1963)

- On May 25, 1963, 31 African states formed a loose organization of African states that would (1) guard independence, (2) promote cooperation, and (3) harmonize social and economic development policies.

- The Organization of African Unity (OAU) was launched.
  - It was the first Pan African intergovernmental organization of independent African countries based on African soil.
  - In the 1990s OAU numbered 53/54 nations with the headquarters in Addis Ababa Ethiopia.

AFRICAN UNION (AU 1999)

- In 1999, African leaders recognized the greater need for collaboration transforming the OAU into the African Union.
- This symbolized African heads of states' need for mobilization to cooperate to solve continental rather than local or regional problems.

- 2002 the AU drafted the "New Partnership for Africa's Development" a blueprint for economic development coordination continentally.

- The AU created its own Human Rights Court, an All-African Parliament, and a Council of African Leaders/ Executive Council.

- In 2003, the Peace & Security Council went into full force.
  - a. It deploys peace-keeping and intervention missions to help in cases of genocide, war crimes, and crimes against humanity.

- Today there are 55 member states.

COLONIAL IMPACT ON AFRICAN ECONOMIES

- Colonialism affected production, distribution, and consumption on the continent. As the Industrial Revolution spread throughout Europe, higher quantities of raw materials were required for production growth in recently established factories.

Primary commodity trade that begun early in the 19th century expanded to include other commodities resulting from successful experimentation with crops introduced from other parts of the world.

- Among these crops were cotton and other fibers introduced for export to new European textile mills. A. Coffee, tea, and cocoa for production of beverages and sweets were other products for wealthy Europeans. B. This brought many African farmers into the cash economy.

- Following European assumption that only men were farmers, production of these crops was introduced mainly to men, even though African women have always been the important farmers.

- Copper, diamond, gold, cobalt, and manganese mines were created in central and southern Africa mainly. A. The labor demand led to distinct patterns of migration to supply labor.

Young men left home and migrated across borders to work in Rhodesia and South African mines. This changed the role of wives and families who were left behind.

- Forced labor was common leading to involuntary migration. A. The increased production of export commodities caused population movement and affected continental infrastructure.

- Roads and railways were built to remove commodities from the interior to the coast for export to Europe. A. They did not connect or integrate countries on the continent which persists today placing a constraint on countries attempting to implement regional economic integration.
- Colonies provided "captive consumers" evident in the special trade preferences set up between colonial powers and their colonies that remain strong today. As African workers entered the money economy, they wanted imported consumer goods not produced locally like bicycles and radios.
- They worked to buy goods and pay required taxes.

- Colonialism did not start off to assist African countries to economically develop; it was for the benefit of European countries.
- By the 1960s, colonial administrations were dismantled continentally, but many economic ties to the former colonial powers remained.

REGIONAL ECONOMIC COOPERATION

African nations have attempted to join together to economically develop.

1. In 1975 the Economic Community of West African States (ECOWAS) was created.

2. In 1980 the Southern African Development Coordination Conference (SADCC) was created; it was renamed the Southern African Development Community (SADC).

3. The Economic Community of Central African States (ECCAS) was created in 1983.

In 1986, the Intergovernmental Authority on Drought and Development (IGADD) in Northeast Africa was created.

In 1989, Union of the Arab Maghreb (UAM) in North Africa was created.

4. In 1993, the Common Market for Eastern & Southern Africa (COMESA) was created.

CURRENT ISSUES

ECONOMICS

- Since the 1960s when most African countries became independent they have experienced persistent economic problems affecting social aspects of development like health, education, and general quality of life.

- The existence of economic growth, even rapid economic growth, does not mean economic development is occurring. Economic growth may increase income inequality in countries if the wealthy control resources and reap the benefits of greater production. Economic growth may also cause environmental degradation in the race to expand production.

- Economic growth is difficult to achieve when population growth is high. Intense population growth would cause the gross national product (GNP) per capita to decline.

- From 1973 to 1982, economies stagnated because the Organization of Petroleum Exporting Countries (OPEC) agreed to dramatically increase oil prices that immediately affected foreign exchange supply to African countries.

The price increase benefited few African petroleum exporters like Nigeria, Gabon, Angola, and Congo by raising their foreign exchange supply.

- The oil crisis was worsened by the Sahelian drought that stretched across the entire region 1972-1973.
    - Hundreds of thousands of refugees fled to cities or sought pastures often across borders of other countries.

- Agricultural production decreased and livestock starved to death.

Another oil crisis occurred in 1978, lower world prices for African primary commodity exports combined with domestic policy deficiencies led to a period of economic decline in the 1980s and first half of the 1990s.

- Immediately following independence into the 1970s, African nations saw the necessity of industrial development which caused the agricultural sector to be ignored. Emphasis was placed on developing industries.

- Most initial efforts were aimed at setting up import substitution industries (ISI) to produce imported goods believed to save foreign exchange.

It was forgotten that if these industries replaced industries that could produce for export, countries would lose the chance to earn foreign exchange required to import necessary capital like technology.

- ISI did not save foreign exchange as anticipated because African countries had to import required production equipment like spare parts and even raw materials for the production process.

The drive to industrialize motivated rural to urban migration, but there were insufficient jobs to absorb the newcomers from the countryside.

- Africa in the 1990s was in an economic crisis characterized by weak agricultural growth, decline in industrial output, poor export production, disintegration of productive and infrastructural facilities, increasing debt, deteriorating social institutions, and environmental destruction.

- Several African nations remain tied to their former colonial rulers economically through trade preferential agreements and bilateral aid. An example of trade preferential agreements is the European Union's ACP (African, Caribbean, and Pacific) countries agreement.

- Their exports continue to be primary commodities and trade (both exports and imports) directed toward the former colonizers.

- They continue to have mono-crop economies where they depend heavily on one commodity for export earnings.

- The strong parts of African economies are often subject to the effects of subsidies the EU has put in place to protect weaker economic sectors of member states, particularly agriculture.

- Africa struggles with being appropriately integrated into the world economic system.

AIDS IN AFRICA

Complicating the problems of population growth and urbanization is AIDS. Africa with only 10% of the world's population has 20-25% of all AIDS infected population. In the mid-1990s the World Health Organization (WHO) raised the estimate to 15 million infected with AIDS.

The central and eastern part of Africa is considered the AIDS belt where most of the cases are located.

Data suggests the period between HIV infection and death from AIDS is much shorter in Africa than in Western Europe - 5 vs. 11 years. Since most Africans are infected in late adolescence or early 20s, many die before 30 years of age (many women infected at younger ages than men die before 25).

Migration and other population movements are a major source of the spread. The disproportionate concentration of males in cities encourages casual and commercial sex.

Casual sex often involving prostitutes (many poor women with no other means to earn a living) is the major factor in HIV transmission. In Lusaka, Zambia and Nairobi, Kenya tests show 90% of the prostitutes have HIV.

Globally, 73 women have HIV per 100 men, but in Africa 110 women have HIV per 100 men. AIDS has also become a number one killer of children being infected by their mothers during or shortly after birth.

AIDS is found mostly in urban areas where it threatens to demolish more educated and skilled young adults upon whom Africa's future depends. The rate of infection in many central African cities is over 40% of the 30-40 year old age group.

In Kinshasa, Democratic Republic of the Congo (DRC) one of the severely affected cities, over 7% of the city's 3 million people are estimated to have AIDS.

Public health campaigns to educate the public, distribute or encourage condom use, safeguard blood supplies, and discourage risky sexual activity have been launched continentally.

Africa is considered to be a pioneer in AIDS prevention resulting from the creation of radio and TV campaigns and efforts to promote safe sex and condom use.

There continue to be too many African countries with limited resources to educate the public, provide condoms, treat sexually transmitted diseases, and safeguard blood supplies.

The toll of death and illness is overwhelming to Africa's limited healthcare system where medical resources are used for prevention and treatment of infected people.

ECONOMIC IMPACT OF AIDS

The greatest impact of AIDS is at the household level, but is also at the national level.

- Those who are HIV positive may have to deal with stigma of infection making it difficult to find employment.

- The death of a spouse may cause family income to decrease dramatically. It can also alter division of labor.
- There is a strong likelihood of both husband and wife dying, leaving increasing numbers of orphans impacting standard of living and educational opportunities.
- The percentage of children born HIV positive will increase as the number of women infected increases.
- Largest number of AIDS cases tends to be among men and women in the most productive age groups leading to a profound impact on labor supply, reducing the size and productivity of the labor force.
- In rural areas, there is a reduction of the number of adults who can produce food.
- Increased cost of hospital and outpatient care and medicine will drive up countries' healthcare budget requirements.

AFRICAN-AMERICAN HISTORY

CIVIL WAR, EMANCIPATION & RECONSTRUCTION

The Civil War & Emancipation

By February 1861, seven slave states, in the Lower South, had seceded from the Union. They chose Jefferson Davis of Mississippi, a former U.S. Senator and Secretary of War, as President.

April 12, 1861 - Confederates started the Civil War by firing on Fort Sumter in Charleston Harbor.

1862 President Abraham Lincoln stated "My paramount object in this struggle is to save the Union and is not either to save or destroy slavery..."

President Lincoln believed that the Confederacy could be defeated rapidly and by usual means with white troops. He feared any attempt to emancipate the slaves would prolong the war.

One month into the war, slaves were escaping to Union lines. May 1861, General Benjamin F. Butler refused to return slaves that entered into his lines; he claimed that because the Confederates were using slaves to build military fortifications, he could keep them as contraband property, subject to confiscation under the rules of war, instead of returning them under the 1850 Fugitive Slave Act.

The importance of slave labor to the Confederacy was illustrated in July 1861 at the First Battle of Bull Run in VA --- the fortifications that helped the Confederates win were built by slaves.

Late in 1861, Lincoln began developing an emancipation program. He tried to avoid offending the slave states in the Union and public opinion generally. November 1861, he sent an emancipation proposal to the Delaware legislature providing for gradual emancipation over a 30-year period, with compensation to masters paid partly by the federal government.

Lincoln also tried to develop a colonization plan to send slaves abroad after emancipation. He shared with many of his time the idea that whites and blacks were better off apart.

At Lincoln's request, Congress in April and July 1862, voted for funds for colonizing freed people. In August Lincoln met with a delegation of Blacks to promote colonization in Central America; Haiti was another place they considered as well.

Even with opposition, public opinion was in favor of freeing and arming the slaves. July 17, 1862 Congress passed the Second Confiscation Act that freed all slaves belonging to those who supported the rebellion. Four days later, Lincoln called his cabinet together and announced that he would issue a proclamation freeing all slaves in those states or parts of states still in rebellion on January 1, 1863.

When Lincoln signed the Emancipation Proclamation on January 1, 1863, he justified it as a military necessity, not as an act of liberation, and he signed it as Commander and Chief of the armed forces, not as President.

The proclamation did cover approximately 3 million slaves in Confederate territory and was an invitation for them to cross over to the Union lines. The proclamation also led to a policy of recruiting Black soldiers.

Some Black units were already organized like the First Regiment Louisiana Native Guards formed in September 1862.

Shortly after the proclamation, Lincoln ordered the enrollment of four regiments of Black infantry and a battalion of Black mounted scouts; recruitment headquarters were set up in New York and New Orleans. In May 1863, the War Department formed the Bureau of Colored Troops to supervise all matters relating to Black units.

Approximately 180,000 Black troops served in the Union Army during the Civil War, almost three-quarters from the slave states; Black units were led almost entirely by White commissioned officers. More than 37,000 were killed in the war.

RECONSTRUCTION

In December 1863, Lincoln announced his "Ten Percent Plan"; for the government of any ex-Confederate state to get Presidential recognition, only 10% of the qualified voters of 1860 would have to swear allegiance to the United States. They could then elect delegates to draw up a new state constitution which had to abolish slavery. After this was accomplished, a new government could be formed. Lincoln's plan made no provision for Black legal and political rights; it assumed Blacks would continue to play their traditional role as subordinates.

In March 1864, Lincoln suggested that the "intelligent Blacks," especially those who fought for the Union, might be allowed to vote. None of the four ex-Confederate states that accepted Lincoln's plan --- VA, TN, LA, and AR made arrangements for Black voting.

After the assassination of Lincoln in April 1865, Vice President Andrew Johnson replaced him. Johnson was a pro-Union Democrat from eastern Tennessee who disliked the South's slaveholding elite, but he was a racist with minimal sympathy for Blacks.

Johnson's approach to reconstruction was similar to Lincoln's; in May 1865, he recognized the four state governments that formed according to Lincoln's plan. That same month he issued his own reconstruction plan.

Johnson's plan pardoned and the restored the property (except slaves) of Confederate supporters willing to take a loyalty oath, with 2 exceptions: major Confederate officials and people with over $20,000 worth of property had to apply individually for pardons. All who took the loyalty oath and who had been qualified to vote in 1860 (meaning Whites only) were eligible to elect delegates to state conventions that would write new constitutions.

The fall 1865 elections gave planters and former Confederate officials control of most of the new governments. The majority of those sent to Congress were Confederate officers.

In December 1865, Johnson announced the end of Reconstruction and issued pardons to those just elected so they could take office.

The Johnson state governments tried to restore Blacks to virtual slavery through laws known as the Black Codes. The Codes legalized Black marriages and permitted Blacks to buy, own, and sell property and to sue or be sued, but stopped them from sitting on juries and from testifying against Whites.

Many codes required Blacks to sign yearly labor contracts and provided for the punishment of those who left their plantations before their contracts expired- to prevent Blacks from bargaining with other employers for better terms.

Vagrancy laws like those of pre-war MD and DE, apprenticeship laws enabling local authorities to take Black children away from supposedly unfit parents and place them with White guardians, and laws permitting leasing out of convicts all were designed to provide Whites with free or cheap Black labor. These governments failed to protect Blacks from acts of violence.

March 1865 Congress created the Bureau of Refugees, Freedmen, and Abandoned Land---known as the Freedmen's Bureau to help former slaves adjust to freedom. It also took control of legal cases involving Blacks. Most moderate Republicans were not yet ready to support voting rights for Blacks. By early 1866, most of them supported legislation promoting social welfare of freed people and assuring them equality before the law.

Congress passed the Civil Rights Act of 1866 which became the 14th Amendment that gave national citizenship to all persons born in the U.S. except indigenous peoples. It also guaranteed citizens equal protection of person and property and authorized U.S. officials to safeguard these rights by bringing suit in federal courts. President Johnson vetoed both bills, but Congress overrode his vetoes.

For the first time in U.S. history Blacks were recognized as citizens with equal rights before the law.

Tennessee ratified the 14th Amendment in 1866, and Congress seated its senators and representatives, completing the state's restoration to the Union. Between October 1866 and January 1867, the legislatures of the other 10 ex-Confederate states rejected the amendment.

Early 1867 Congress gave the vote to Blacks in Washington D.C. and in the territories. In the First Reconstruction Act of March 1867 and in three later acts, Congress spelled out its plan for Radical Reconstruction.

In each state voters were to choose delegates to a state convention that would write a constitution that must contain a clause guaranteeing the vote to all adult males. After the people ratified the constitution, they were to elect a state government.

By 1868 six states ---NC, SC, FL, AL, LA, AR had been restored to the Union after meeting these terms. Four states VA, GA, MS, and TX did not meet the terms before the 14th Amendment became part of the U.S. Constitution in 1868.

The 15th Amendment was ratified and sent to those four states in February 1869, it prohibited both the federal and state governments from denying anyone the vote "on account of race, color, or previous condition of servitude." It became law in 1870.

Most supporters of Radical Reconstruction thought that granting land to the freed people was the next step to fully ensuring the rights of Blacks. For example, Representative Thaddeus Stevens (PA) argued that Blacks would not be able to defend their new rights without the economic independence of land ownership.

In 1866 and 1867 Stevens, Senator Charles Sumner (MA) and Representatives George W. Julian (IN) and Benjamin F. Butler (MA) proposed legislation to break up large plantations owned by Confederate supporters and give part of the land to Blacks. Congress rejected their proposals by wide margins. Moderate and Radical Republicans believed that the right to vote would be enough to enable Blacks to defend their civil and political rights.

Many landowners attempted to restore the old gang-labor system on plantations, it would maintain high White supervision. Blacks resisted so many planters broke up large gangs into smaller groups.

Under pressure from freed people, some planters introduced the share cropping system by 1866; each Black family took responsibility for a piece of land and received a share of the crop grown on it. This system made White supervision difficult. By 1880 more Blacks worked on a sharecropping basis than as wage laborers.

Governments elected under Constitutions

In the late 1860s and early 1870s, a high proportion of Black public officials were freeborn; by the mid-1870s the proportion of freed people had begun growing, thanks in part to the education they received in the new school systems and self-confidence it inspired.

Blacks held office at every level, though in low proportion to their overall populations. Among the first Blacks elected to Congress → Republicans

Senator Hiram R. Revels (1869- 1871) Mississippi

Rep. Benjamin S. Turner (1871-1873) Alabama

Rep. Josiah T. Walls (1871-1877) Florida

Rep. Joseph H. Rainey (1869-1879) South Carolina

Rep. Robert B. Elliot (1871-1875) South Carolina

Rep. Robert C. De Large (1871-1873) South Carolina

Rep. Jefferson H. Long (1869-1871) Georgia

The Freedmen's Bureau

Commissioner General Oliver O. Howard.

Officers issued clothing, food, medicine to destitute refugees and freedmen. They established hospitals, schools, and employment offices, and camps for the homeless. They registered marriages, helped Black veterans file and collect claims for bounties, pensions, and back pay. They also oversaw writing of labor contracts.

The Bureau was the first social welfare bureaucracy created by the federal government and was an example of the expanding role of the federal government into state affairs.

96

Funding for the Bureau came from the sale and rent of land. It was authorized to rent abandoned and confiscated property to freedmen for three years.

At the end of the Civil War, more than 800,000 acres reverted to the Bureau, during 1865 more than half that land was rented to freedmen. By the fall of 1865 almost all of the land that the Bureau controlled on behalf of freedmen was returned to pre-war owners.

With no land sales or rents, the Bureau no longer had a source of funding and no longer actively promoted Black ownership of land. Freedmen were forced back to the plantations where they entered contracts that exchanged labor for money or crops. The Bureau's main duty changed to overseeing these contracts.

Freedmen were required to be under contract, if they broke the contract they would be imprisoned.

The Bureau did a lot of work in education. The second Freedmen's Bureau Act of July 13, 1866 authorized funds for salaries of state superintendents of education and for the repair and rental of school buildings. The Bureau also built school houses or found buildings large enough to seat 40-50 students-in a church, stable, someone's house, and abandoned buildings.

The Bureau's policy prohibited paying for books and teachers' salaries, so Black families were required to furnish board and at least $30 a month for a teacher before opening a school.

Eventually, teachers and technical colleges and universities were established by the Bureau to train Black teachers, preachers, and doctors. Some of these schools were Atlanta University (American Missionary Association collaborated with the Bureau to establish this school), Fisk University, Hampton University, and Howard University (named after the Bureau's commissioner).

President Johnson and several men in prominent positions, did not believe Blacks should have their own bureau or that money should be spent to help Blacks move from slavery to freedom. He *began his attacks on the Bureau a year after it was founded by vetoing the second Freedmen's Bureau Act 1866 that would extend its operations for two more years and give it an adequate budget.*

As a result of high costs, limited budgets, corruption, excessive patronage, White opposition and no support from the President, the Bureau discontinued its existence in 1870.

AFRICANS IN AMERICA IN THE 21ST CENTURY

EDUCATION

Several African-American students choose to attend historically Black colleges and universities (HBCUs); they account for a significant number of African-American graduates.

According to the U.S Department of Education fall enrollment at HBCUs at two year and four year schools stood at 274,212 students in 1999. In 1964 over 51% of all African-Americans in college were still enrolled in HBCUs, by 1970 the proportion was 28%, fall 1978 16.5% and 6.2% 1998.

As recently as 1999-2000 24% of all African-Americans receiving Bachelor's degrees receive them from HBCUs.

Studies show recently 40% of adult African-American males are functionally illiterate and the number of incarcerated men outnumbers the number of men on college and university campuses.

98

Some mainstream institutions have seen a decrease in the number of Black students enrolled; CUNY has launched a system wide African-American male initiative aimed to 'improve the success and retention of Black men on its 11 senior college campuses.'

Afro-centrism is based on the belief that ancient Greeks stole the most of the great philosophical and mathematical thoughts from Egyptians who are an African people. The Greek philosopher Aristotle got much of his work from the plundered Egyptian city of Alexandria they believe that Socrates was actually Black.

Afro-centrists claim the educational system is flawed and promoted white supremacy. It teaches history, arts, science, and other disciplines from a traditional European viewpoint. African contributions to these fields are completely ignored or given inadequate attention.

They favor teaching African-American children from an Afro-centric point of view by championing Black culture, history, achievement which will increase their self-worth and give them greater sense of identity and pride.

Afro-centrism is not a new phenomenon it was supported in the early 20th century by Marcus Garvey and Carter G. Woodson.

The nation has seen an increase in the number of single gender schools' one is the Young Women's Leadership School in East Harlem opened fall 1996. YMLS started with 56 7th grade girls and has expanded to 360 students in grades 7-12 by the year 2000. Studies found that girls perform better academically without the presence of boys.

EMPLOYMENT

Historically, including much of the 20th century, African-Americans were restricted to service jobs in all industry sectors.

African-Americans were locked out of professional sports and restricted to segregated leagues, ignored in arts, and not considered seriously as politicians. By 2002, while still underrepresented, African-Americans headed major corporations and sat on corporate boards of directors.

African-Americans have increasingly made strides in production and executive positions in the film industry.

Employment opportunities have improved, but the effects of race are not completely gone.

The growing African-American middle class experienced a greater range of occupational and economic opportunities than ever before, but an increasing number of African-Americans who are disadvantaged were locked out of the mainstream of American life.

March 2000, there were approximately 16 million African-Americans or 12% of the civilian labor force. The participation rate for Black men is 68.1% and Black women 63.9%. White men's participation rate 74.3% and White women 60.8%. Black men were less likely to be in job market than White men.

Unemployment remains a problem among African-Americans in the labor force. During the early 1990s the unemployment rate for African-Americans fluctuated but remained above 11%. Not until 1995, the unemployment rate for African-Americans dropped below 11%. In 1997, the unemployment rate was 10%, by 1999 unemployment rate declined to 9%.

January 2008- 9.4%; January 2009- 13.4%; 2X Whites- 2008 - 4.9%; 2009- 7.8%.

17% of employed Black males maintained jobs in the lower-paying service sector compared to 8% of White males. Operators, fabricators, and laborers category was the largest occupation group for Black men; the managerial and professional category was the largest single category for White men.

The change from manufacturing-based economy to highly computerized and information based- economy had an effect on blue-collar work. Together with experience of racial restrictions, the higher number of less-skilled African-American workers suffered the most.

This was complicated for less-skilled, inner-city African-Americans who were geographically isolated from the growing number of jobs that shifted to the suburbs and socially isolated from informal job networks that have become a major source of job placement.

Racial discrimination maintains disparity between Blacks and Whites even when education levels are the same. Sociological studies have consistently shown that Blacks with comparable levels of education, occupation, and experience tend to earn less than their White counterparts.

Black men with a high school diploma earn 76% of the income of high school educated White men. Black men with a bachelor's degree earn 75% of the amount their White counterparts; those with professional degrees earn 61%; at the doctoral level, Black men earn only 54% as much as White men with the same education.

In 1999, Black men with a doctorate averaged less income than White men with a bachelor's degree.

Government statistics on poverty showed a 20% decrease in the number of African-Americans in poverty since 1960.

In 1996, the poverty rate for Whites was 9.6% while the poverty rate for Blacks was 26.1%. By 2005, the poverty rate for Whites fell to 8.6% while the poverty rate for Blacks declined to 22.1%. The reality is that the proportion of Blacks living at or below the poverty line is nearly three times as great as Whites.

Some 10.1 million African-Americans were near poor in 2000; the severely poor, the poor, and the near poor comprised 33% of the African-American population.

Some have advocated self-help to improve the situation of African-Americans because social intervention programs are not likely to be initiated by the federal government.

POLICE BRUTALITY

Two white officers (current and former) in Inglewood, Ca. were acquitted of felony charges in the beating of teenager Donovan Jackson and allegedly covering it up. *Los Angeles Sentinel July 31, 2003.*

Community members were assaulted by police after a police car carrying a prisoner collided with another car in Bedford Stuyvesant Brooklyn; when the EMT arrived they attended to the minor injured officers instead of the people who were more seriously injured. The community expressed concern and defended those people. Every type of police vehicle came, helicopters hovered, and some police came wearing black gloves with shot guns pointed toward people saying "you want some of this?" They began pushing and assaulting people who were standing by and jumped people ten on one. Eight people were arrested and taken to the 79th precinct. *Big Red News June 15-21, 2006*

Latoya Brown, 24 year old African-American woman was assaulted by police officer Mark Deters on September 17, 2006 in Ottawa Hills. He was allowed to resign nine days after meaning his record will be clean. Ms. Brown dropped off four 13 year olds whom she had driven to a youth-oriented musical concert in Detroit. She was driving her father home who had been drinking, when they were stopped by Deters who smelled alcohol. He gave Ms. Brown a series of sobriety tests even after the Breathalyzer showed she had not been drinking. He gave her such tests as watching his moving finger and instructed to keep her head still, reciting the middle letters of the alphabet and counting backward from 67 to 43. When counting backward she stopped at 47, Deters became irritated and said what did I tell you to count to? Brown said she thought he said 47. What made him angry was her throwing the speeding citation out of the window; she was irritated by the fact he held her up a long time and it was established from the initial stop that she had not been drinking. She took the ticket threw it out and said "don't throw anything at me." Deters opened the door to the car grabbed her out and slammed her up against the side of the SUV. He grabbed the back of her hair and threw her down, put his knee in her back, and pulled her arms behind her back to arrest her. This was all caught on his police car video. Ms. Brown's father got out stood away and called to the officer to stop, but feared for his life. He told Deters "don't do that… you don't have to do her like that." Deters made a motion for his gun; Mr. Brown feared for his life. He himself is a former Mississippi state police trooper and security officer as well as President of the advocacy group

102

African-American Parents Association. *Chicago Weekend October 25, 2006.*

Joint project of Color Lines and the Chicago Reporter analyzed police shootings form 2000-2005 for ten cities across the U.S.: San Antonio, Las Vegas, San Diego, New York, Dallas, Philadelphia, Los Angeles, Chicago, Phoenix, and Houston. Each city has a population of more than 1 million. In all 10 cities the percentage of Black shooting victims is higher than the percentage of Black people in the population. In NY, San Diego, and Las Vegas, the percentage of Black people killed is at least double their share of the city's total population. *Big Red News November 15-21, 2007.*

Stanley Howard, Madison Hobley, Leroy Orange, and Aaron Patterson will split $19.8 million after they sued the city of Chicago claiming former Police Commissioner Jon Burge and his fellows tortured them into making false confessions. These men were part of the Death Row 10 who alleged Burge used electric shock, cattle prods, and placed a plastic typewriter bag over their heads to get the false confessions. These men were pardoned by the Former Governor George Ryan in 2003. Leroy Orange endured 12 hours of questioning at Area 2 headquarters where he was shocked with wires attached to his buttocks, testicles, and arms and suffocated with a plastic bag over head. He spent 19 years in jail, 14 of which were on death row because of the false confession. *Chicago Weekend January 16, 2008.*

Sitting in his SUV in Corona Queens May 2, 2008, Chief Zeigler head of the Community Affairs Bureau since January 2006 was approached by two White officers, one of them with his gun drawn. They ordered him out of the vehicle and refused to acknowledge his identification. Zeigler is the city's highest ranking Black police officer. If he made one wrong move he would have been dead. *Sacramento Observer May 22-28, 2008.*

103

SECTION 3 POLITICAL SCIENCE AND CIVIC ENGAGEMENT

AMERICAN GOVERNMENT AND POLITICS

BRANCHES OF GOVERNMENT

Legislative Branch → Congress
- 535 members [100 Senators & 435 Representatives] – only federal officials elected directly by the people.
- Session almost year round, during a 2 yr. session, consider 12,000 bills on a number of issues.

- Typical day- members divide time between
- committee meetings
- sessions within the House or Senate
- meetings with constituents, lobbyists
- visiting dignitaries

- 1st Congress 1789-1790, each Congress serves for a 2 yr. term, meets in 2 sessions, assembling on or soon after January 3.

Some of the major delegated or enumerated powers include:
- Levying & collecting taxes
- Borrowing money
- Coining money & regulating its value
- Regulating interstate & foreign trade
- Granting patents & copyrights
- Declaring war
- Raising & supporting an army & navy
- Creating courts below the Supreme Court
- Using state militias to execute the nation's laws
- Creating post offices
- Controlling naturalization of immigrants
- Controlling federal property within the states

- Make all laws necessary & proper for carrying into execution the foregoing powers – elastic clause.

- Primary function – legislative – make laws that govern the nation.
- Except for money bills (appropriation), any bill can be introduced by any member of Congress.
- Only a small % of bills become law.
- House and Senate each have jurisdiction over certain areas of public policy.
- If a bill makes it through the debate of its committee, it will go on to be considered by the chamber of Congress in which it was initiated.

Congressional Checks on the Executive
- May impeach & remove President from office
- May override President's veto
- Senate can refuse to ratify treaties & confirm appointments

Congressional Checks on the Judicial
- Impeach & remove judges
- Refuse judicial appointments
- Propose constitutional amendments
- Create lower courts
- Regulate Supreme Court's jurisdiction

Executive Branch → President
- Combined roles of:
- Chief of state
- Chief diplomat
- Commander-in-Chief of the armed forces
- Chief executive
- Chief legislator
- Head of his/her political party
- Has only powers implied by the Constitution.

- Presidential election – 2 races →
- (1) Nominated by his/her political party.

- (2) Win the national election for office of the President.
- George Washington was unanimously chosen by the Electoral College (state electors responsible for electing the President) as President.
- John Adams, Thomas Jefferson, James Madison, & James Monroe were all nominated by party leaders in Congress → congressional caucus.
- People voiced opposition to this practice as a violation of the Constitution & separation of powers.
- Part of democratic reforms of the Jackson era (1820-1840), national nominating convention was developed →
- Delegates from different states gather to nominate a candidate.
- Permitted more citizen participation in the nomination of a party candidate.
- Today – delegates are selected for the national convention through the caucus method or primary method (voters choose candidates to represent the political parties in the general election) within states.
- Every 4 years, on the 1st Tuesday after the 1st Monday in November, citizens vote for electors pledged to 1 presidential candidate or another.
- Executive branch has been expanded
- Today the President is helped by 2.6 million civilian employees working in departments, agencies, boards, and commissions.

- 1- Department of the State (created 1789)
- 2- Department of the Treasury (1789)
- 3- Department of Justice (1789)
- 4- Department of the Interior (1849)
- 5- Department of Agriculture (1889)
- 6- Department of Commerce (1903)
- 7- Department of Labor (1913)
- 8- Department of Defense (1947)
- 9- Department of Health & Human Services (1953)
- 10- Department of Housing & Urban Development (1965)
- 11- Department of Transportation (1966)

- 12- Department of Energy (1977)
- 13- Department of Education (1979)
- 14- Department of Veterans Affairs (1988)
- 15- Department of Homeland Security (2002)

Executive Checks on the Legislative
- Veto laws
- Call special sessions of Congress
- Propose laws

Executive Checks on the Judicial
- Grant pardons & exonerations
- Appoints Supreme Court justices & other federal judges

Judicial Branch → Supreme Court
- The court has the authority to create lower courts.
- Congress passed the Judiciary Act of 1789 –
- established 13 district courts in major cities
- 3 circuit courts
- 1 Supreme Court with a Chief Justice & 5 Associates.
- Supreme Court has 9 justices today.

- Supreme Court is granted
- Original jurisdiction - the right to hear a case for the 1st time.
- Appellate jurisdiction – the right to accept & hear cases coming from lower federal courts & the highest state courts.
- When the Supreme Court agrees to hear a case on appeal from a lower court, it is said that the Court is granting certiorari.
- Reviews the constitutionality of legislative acts.

- The idea of judicial review (court's power to determine if executive and Congress's acts are in accordance with the Constitution) stems from the principles of limited government.

- Chief Justice John Marshall's (1755-1835) opinion in the Supreme Court case of Marbury v. Madison 1803 established the precedent for judicial review.
- The Court upheld part of the Judiciary Act of 1789, an act of Congress, to be unconstitutional (contrary to the constitution).

- Twelve (12) regional federal judicial courts serve the U.S.
- Each court has its own court of appeals & a different number of district (trial) courts- total 94.
- Each state has its own judicial structure with trial courts, courts of appeal, & a highest court of final state appeal.
- Only a small % of cases seeking Supreme Court review are accepted.

Judicial Checks on the Executive
- May declare executive acts unconstitutional
- Supreme Court justices are appointed for life & are free from executive control

Judicial Checks on the Legislative
- May declare laws of Congress unconstitutional

POLITICS OF ECONOMICS: INTRODUCTION TO POLITICAL ECONOMY

WHAT IS GOVERNMENT?

What is political science?

Study of the:
- State/government/political systems or structures
- Political practices
- Political behavior
- Politics → power → government (state) → head of state → representatives → elections → interests groups

- Politics → activities connected to control of public decisions among a people or territory.
- Politics → the shaping of these decisions, who gets to make them, & for what purposes.
- System → (1) a set of mutually dependent parts & (2) boundaries toward its environment.
- Political system → the whole group of related institutions & agencies that make decisions & policies for a people or territory.
- Government → organization of individuals who have the power to make binding decisions on behalf of a particular community.

Governments have authoritative & coercive powers; they can:
- wage war or promote peace
- encourage or restrict international trade
- tax their populations
- distribute resources for education, health, and welfare

Government's purposes also include:
- providing security & maintaining order
- protecting rights
- promoting economic productivity & growth
- promoting social justice
- protecting the weak

- Sovereignty → political independence from any higher authority. → Freedom from outside control.
- Nation-state → national identifications & sovereign political authority coincide – the state (government) is made up of individuals who share a common national identity.
- Monarchy → a political system in which power rests in one person or monarch (King/Queen) usually acquired through heredity.
- Constitutional monarchy → limited monarchy or political system where a monarch is bound and must adhere to a constitution which limits his/her power.

- Democracy → idea of a governing body by & for the people.
- The type of political system a nation has with free & fair elections and levels of participation.
- Republic → a political system where supreme power is placed in the citizens who elect representatives that exercise power on their behalf.
- These representatives are accountable to the citizens.
- A political system in which the head of state is elected or nominated.
- Communism → economic system in which a single party controls the means of production with the goal of creating a classless society.
- Despotism → a political system where rule is absolute, tyrannical, and in cases, brutal (can be in the hands of 1 person or group).
- Authoritarian government → a political system that allows little or no participation in decision making by individuals & groups outside the top levels of government.

ECONOMICS DEFINED

- A social science that studies how individuals, governments, & firms make choices on allocating scarce/limited resources to satisfy their unlimited wants.
- Economics can be broken down into:
- Macroeconomics → examines the behavior of the total economy.
- Microeconomics → focuses on individual consumers.

- Physiocrats → French thinkers during the Enlightenment era who wrote about economics.
- Leader of the Physiocrats, Francois Quesnay (1694-1774) taught that economics had its own set of natural laws.
- *The most basic of these laws was that of supply & demand.*

- These laws operated with little governmental regulation of private economic activity.
- Laissez-faire (French for allow/ let do) or noninterference.
- They supported free trade & enterprise.
- They thought the key source of national wealth was land & agriculture.

- Mercantilism → 17th century theory that trading states/countries should increase their wealth & power by expanding exports & protecting their domestic economy from imports.
- Amount of wealth in the world was fixed by the amount of precious metals (gold & silver).
- Countries should export more than they import.
- Another understanding/interpretation of mercantilism includes the idea that states/countries must protect their own interests at the expense of others.

- Adam Smith (1723-1790) Wealth of Nations (1776)
- Central issues → productivity of labor & how it is used.
- Mercantile restrictions like high taxes on imports didn't encourage productive distribution of labor – doesn't create economic health.
- General prosperity could be achieved by allowing the "invisible hand" to lead economic activity.
- Individuals should pursue their own interests without competition from state approved monopolies or legal restrictions.

- Capitalism developed during the 18th and 19th centuries during industrialization.
- Capitalism → Economic system where the means of production & distribution are privately owned.
- The central aspect → profit.
- The focus is on individual effort/enterprise.
- Property- owners of the means of production (factories, land, tools, and machines) are called capitalists.

3 Conditions are necessary for pure capitalism to exist:

- *Private property ownership* → individuals are encouraged to own property including capital necessary to produce & distribute goods & services.
- *Personal profit* → individuals are allowed to maximize their personal gains.
- *Competition* → mechanism that determines what is produced & at what price.
- 4th requirement → *government policy of laissez-faire* → allowing the marketplace to run without restrictions.
- Some argue that government involvement would distort the economy by negatively affecting incentives & freedom of individual choice.
- Critics argue that capitalism promotes inequality because profit is the object, not improvement of the human condition.

- Market economy → an economic system in which economic decisions & pricing of goods & services are guided only by the interactions of a country's citizens & businesses.
- There is little government intervention or central planning.

- Industrialization → a process of economic expansion through the development of industries in which new power sources & technologies are used.
- This allows for much faster production & higher quantity of finished/manufactured goods.
- 5 necessities :
- Natural resources/ raw materials
- Labor force/ Human resources
- Available capital (land, tools, factories, machines)
- Available markets (places to sell & buy goods)
- Favorable government

- Communism and socialism Karl Marx (1818-1883) Communist Manifesto (1848)

- Communism → economic system in which a single party controls the means of production with the goal of creating a classless society.
- Socialism → a system of social organization where the means of production & distribution were held by the people/community.
- Capitalism involves too much exploitation.
- Working class/proletariat will eventually revolt against the capitalists.
- Revolution's result → a utopian like society, one without classes.

5 Principles of Socialism:
- *Democratic habits* → true socialism must be democratic; representatives of a socialist state must answer & be responsive to the public they serve.
- Key thing to remember: nations that claim to be socialist but are authoritarian, violate this basic aspect of socialism.
- *Egalitarianism* → equality of opportunity for self-fulfillment of all.
- Equality in sharing the benefits of society.
- Achieving this by leveling out major inequalities in income, poverty, & opportunities.
- *Community* → cooperation & sense of collective belonging.
- *Public ownership of means of production* → people own the basic industries, financial institutions, utilities, transportation, & communication companies.
- *Planning for common purposes* → to meet citizens' material needs.

- Command economy → A system where the government determines:
- what goods should be produced
- how much should be produced
- price at which the goods will be offered for sale
- The command economy is a key feature of any communist society.

113

- China, Cuba, North Korea & the former Soviet Union are examples of countries that have command economies.

- John Maynard Keynes (1883-1946) British economist & major contributor to macroeconomics.
- Opposed Say's Law (Jean-Baptiste Say, economist & businessman) which said supply creates demand.
- Keynes understood the opposite to be true – demand creates supply.
- Unemployment results from people not spending enough.
- In recessions, aggregate demand of economies fall.
- Aggregate demand → total amount of goods & services demanded in an economy at a given price & time.
- Businesses & people spend less $ → demand falls → job losses → falls in spending.
- Solution → governments should borrow $ & boost demand by pushing $ into the economy.
- When the economy recovers, the government should repay loans.
- Successful economies have contributions from both the government & private sector.
- Government should take part in economic management.
- Keynes' Books →
- The Economic Consequences of the Peace (1919)
- A Treatise on Probability (1921)
- A Tract on Monetary Reform (1923)
- A Treatise on Money (1930)
- The General Theory of Employment, Interest and Money (1936)

MACROECONOMICS[4]

National Economy

- The study of a nation's economy as a whole.

- Focus on issues of:

  - Inflation

  - Unemployment

  - Economic growth

  - Trade

  - Gross domestic product

CONCEPTS

- Inflation → continued increases in the average prices of all goods & services.

- Gross Domestic Product (GDP) → total value of all newly produced goods & services in a country in a given year.

- GDP Per capita → the average income of people in a country.

- Real GDP → a measure of GDP that controls for changes in prices.

- Nominal GDP → the value of GDP in current dollars.

- Economic growth → continued increases in the real GDP of an economy over a long period of time.

- MEASURES of GDP

---

[4] This information was taken from a book of readings assembled by the faculty of the Business Department at Kingsborough Community College, CUNY for an introductory economics course offered in that department in 2012.

- Consumption expenditure → purchases of newly produced goods & services by people.

- Private investment expenditure → purchases of newly produced goods & services by companies.

- Government expenditure → purchases of newly produced goods & services by local, state & federal governments.

- Net exports → exports minus imports.

- Trade deficit → the excess of imports.

- Trade surplus → the excess of exports.

- National income → total income earned by a nation's residents in the production of goods & services both domestically & abroad.

- Gross National Product → GDP plus net income earned abroad.

- Recession → 6 consecutive months of declining GDP.

- Peak → the date at which a recession starts.

- Trough → the date at which output stops falling in a recession.

- Expansion → period after a trough in the business cycle when the economy recovers.

- Depression → severe recession.

PRODUCTION & INCOME

- Production & income – crucial to a nation's economic health.

- Production creates income.

- Income leads to production.

- Households (consumers) & firms (companies) make transactions in 2 markets →

  - (1) factor markets

  - (2) product markets

- In *factor* (input) *markets*, households (consumers) supply labor to firms (companies).

- In the end, households own firms & all of the resources firms use in production are called capital.

- Households (consumers) provide capital (land, buildings, & equipment) to firms to produce output.

- *Product* (output) *markets* are markets in which companies sell goods & services to consumers.

- In factor markets, when households (consumers) supply labor & capital to firms they are paid by the firms (companies).

- They earn wages for their work, & they earn interest, dividends, & rents on the capital they supply to the firms (companies).

- Households (consumers) use their income to buy goods & services in the product markets.

- The firm (company) uses the revenue it gets from selling its products to pay for the elements of production (land, labor, & capital).

- When goods & services are produced income flows throughout the economy.

- For example, when a computer is manufactured and sold income is created through its production.

- The manufacturer pays wages to workers, pays rent on offices & factory buildings, & pays interest on $ borrowed from a bank.

- Whatever is left is the firm's (company's) profit.

117

- Wages, rent, interest & profits → various forms of income.

SHORTCOMINGS OF GDP

- GDP doesn't take 4 things into account :

    - Housework & childcare → ignores transactions that don't take place in organized markets. → Services like cleaning, cooking, providing free childcare, things people do for themselves in their homes.

    - Leisure → GDP is designed to measure the production that occurs in the economy.

    - Underground economy → ignores transactions unreported to official authorities.

    - Pollution → GDP does not value environmental changes that occur in production of output.

        - Example – factory produces $1,000 of output, but pollutes a river & lowers its value by $2,000.

UNEMPLOYMENT

- During periods of poor economic performance & slow growth unemployment rises.

- Even in times of good economic growth unemployment falls but doesn't disappear.

- Labor force → total number of workers, both the employed & unemployed.

- The unemployed are individuals who don't currently have a job, but are actively looking for work.

- *Actively looking* – is important – those who don't have a job & aren't looking for work aren't counted as unemployed.

- Unemployment rate → the number of unemployed divided by the total labor force, it represents a percentage of the labor force.

- Unemployment rate = unemployed/labor force X 100

- Labor force includes those 16 years & older

- Countries in which support is the most generous → less incentive to work & unemployment will tend to be higher.

- This is the case even among industrialized countries.

- The difference factors in government support for unemployed workers.

- For example, in 2006, Belgium had a 10.3% unemployment rate, while Japan had a rate of 4%.

Alternative measures

- Marginally attached workers → divided into 2 groups

  - (1) Discouraged workers → workers who left the labor force because they couldn't find jobs.

  - (2) Workers who aren't looking for work for other reasons like lack of transportation or childcare.

- There are workers employed part-time but would like full-time jobs.

TYPES OF UNEMPLOYMENT

- *Seasonal unemployment* → attached to seasonal factors. For example, farm workers, construction workers in the winter, teenage workers looking for work early summer.

- *Cyclical unemployment* → occurs during changes in real GDP. (falling GDP, companies lay off workers)

119

- *Frictional unemployment* → occurs in the normal workings of the economy, such as workers taking time to search for suitable jobs & companies taking time to search for qualified employees. (when people change jobs, move, take time to find the right job)

- *Structural unemployment* → occurs when there is a mismatch of skills & jobs. (jobs eliminated, new ones created – i.e. change from vinyl records to CDs in the 1980s))

NATURAL RATE OF UNEMPLOYMENT

- *Natural rate of unemployment* → level of unemployment with only *frictional* & *structural* unemployment.

- Full employment → level of unemployment that occurs when the unemployment rate is at the natural rate.

- *The economy actually needs some frictional unemployment to function efficiently.*

- Frictional unemployment exists so that workers & companies can find appropriate employment matches.

Inflation

- Inflation rate → percentage rate of change in the price level.

- Deflation → negative inflation or falling prices of goods & services.

- Anticipated inflation → inflation that is expected.

- Unanticipated inflation → inflation that is unexpected.

- Hyperinflation → an inflation rate that exceeds 50% per month.

BIBLIOGRAPHY

WORLD HISTORY, AFFAIRS, AND CULTURES

Cole, Joshua and Carol Symes. *Western Civilizations: Their History & Their Culture.* New York: W. W. Norton & Company, 2013.

Bova, Russell. *How the World Works: A Brief Survey of International Relations.* London:Pearson, 2010.

Eitzen, D. Stanley, Kelly Eitzen Smith, and Maxine Baca Zinn. *Social Problems.* London: Pearson, 2011.

Frankforter, A. Daniel and William M. Spellman. *The West: a Narrative History Volume 2 since1400.* London: Pearson, 2013.

Goldstein, Joshua S. and Jon C. Pevehouse. *International Relations.* New York: Longman, 2011.

Lamy, Steven, John Masker, John Baylis, Steve Smith, and Patricia Owens. *Introduction to Global Politics.* Oxford: Oxford University Press, 2014.

McKay, John, Bennett Hill, John B., Patricia B. Ebrey, Roger Beck, Clare Crowston, Merry Wiesner- Hanks. *A History of World Societies Volume 2: Since 1500.* New York: Bedford St. Martin's, 2009.

Salisbury, Joyce and Dennis Sherman. *The West in the World. Volume II from 1600.* New York: McGraw-Hill, 2008.

Collins, Robert O. *Africa a Short History.* Princeton, NJ: Markus Weiner Publishers, 2008.

Davidson, Basil. *West Africa before the Colonial Era: a*

History to 1850. New York: Addison Wesley Longman Publishers, 1998.

Dickerson, Donna L. "The Freedmen's Bureau 1865-72." *The*

African American Experience. http://aae.greenwood.com (Accessed 2009)

Ehret, Christopher *Civilizations of Africa a History to 1800,*

Charlottesville, VA: University of Virginia Press, 2002.

Gilbert, Erik and John T. Reynolds. *Africa in World History:*

From Prehistory to the Present. London: Pearson, 2012.

Gordon, April and Donald Gordon. *Understanding*

Contemporary Africa. London: Reiner Publishers, 1996.

Harris, Joseph E. *Africans and their History.* New York:

Penguin, 2005.

Henson, Verna J. and Michael D. Woodard. "Employment."

Narins, Brigham, Ed. *The African American Almanac.* Detroit, London, New Haven, San Francisco, 2008.

Levine, Michael L. "The Civil War and Black Military

Service." *The African American Experience.* http://aae.greenwood.com (Accessed 2009)

Postma, Johannes. *The Atlantic slave Trade.* Connecticut:

Greenwood Press, 2003.

Smith, Jessie Carney. "Education." Narins, Brigham, Ed. *The*

African American Almanac. Detroit, London, New Haven, San Francisco, 2008.

West-Duran, Alan, ed. *African Caribbeans*. Connecticut:

Greenwood Press, 2003.

POLITICS AND CIVIC ENGAGEMENT

Edwards, George C., Martin P Wattenberg, and Robert L.

Lineberry. *Government in America:People, Politics, and Policy.* London: Pearson, 2011.

About the Author

Candice Rowser began her career as an educator in 2005 with the New York City Department of Education as a Substitute Teacher in the Bronx and Manhattan. She was a part-time faculty member of the City University of New York (CUNY) from 2008 until 2018, first as a Continuing Education Teacher at LaGuardia Community College, and later an Adjunct Assistant Professor. From 2009 until 2010 Dr. Rowser taught at Westchester Community College, State University of New York (SUNY). From 2010 to 2018, she taught college level courses at three CUNY campuses including Kingsborough Community College, Hunter College, and Bronx Community College. Dr. Rowser taught briefly at her alma mater, St John's University, following her graduation in 2010. She taught African-American history part-time at Fordham University for the 2018-2019 academic year.

Dr.Rowser studied at St. John's University completing the Doctor of Arts Modern World History program. She was exposed to anthropology, sociology, political science, economics, and religious studies and learned how these fields contribute to the knowledge and grasp of historical events. She earned her Master's degree in Africana Studies from the University at Albany, SUNY and her Bachelor's degree in History with a minor in Caribbean and Latin American Studies from St Lawrence University. Her research interests include global human rights, particularly the experiences of marginalized communities.